PORTLAND UNDERCOVER

HOW TO VISIT NEW ENGLAND'S HIPPEST CITY WITHOUT LOOKING LIKE A TOURIST.

BY **CHRIS BARRY**

SIGNS YOU'RE A TOURIST IN PORTLAND

YOU WEAR A FANNY PACK.

YOU ACTUALLY SPEAK TO THE SAFARI-HAT WEARING DOWNTOWN GUIDES.

YOU WEAR CLOTHING ADORNED WITH CUTE LOBSTERS AND LIGHTHOUSES.

YOU ASK THE WAITER OR WAITRESS TO HELP TIE A LOBSTER BIB AROUND YOUR NECK.

YOU WONDER WHY ALL THE FISHERMEN PARK THEIR BOATS IN THE SAME DIRECTION.*

*Moored boats all point into the wind and tide.

CASCO BAY WEEKLY
PORTLAND, MAINE

Illustrations by Patrick Corrigan
Layout and Design by Joanna Amato
Editor: Claire Z.Cramer
Maps by Rusty Nelson
All from Portland, of course!

A DISCLAIMER

Prices change often with the seasons and so does travel information. Great entrepreneurs sometimes retire or go south. Businesses close, new ones spring up. No one can guarantee the quality of a travel experience. For this reason neither the author nor the publisher can be held liable for the experiences of our readers. But you are invited to write to the publisher with comments and suggestions for future editions.

Casco Bay Weekly
Maine Publishing Corp
561 Congress Street
Portland, Maine 04101

SPECIAL SALES

Bulk purchase (5 copies or more) are available through Casco Bay Weekly at special discount. And if you like the book and want updates, you might also want to subscribe to our lively alternative weekly. 800-286-6601 cbwpub@maine.rr.com

ACKNOWLEDGMENTS

Thank you for buying this book.
Thanks to all my great Portland friends and neighbors.
Thanks to the folks at CBW, including Lael Morgan and the
rest of the gang who asked me to write about my favorite city.
To Claire Cramer for copy editing and Joanna Amato for designing the book.

I'm extremely grateful to the following Portlanders:
Al Diamon and Lou Ann Clifford for being themselves. John McDonald for professional guidance. Steve Bither, my rock star attorney, for legal advice. The bad boys down at Masterpiece Reprographics for excellent photocopies. Derrick Rancourt and Jennifer Bailey and Gary Race and Marti Lay for being great neighbors. Sawyer and the hippies at Kathleen's Green Machine, Portland's only recycling couriers. John Johnson for stock tips. Dan, the Top Secret Bike Messenger from Outer Space, for believing in alien abductions. Wellspring Spa for massage and attempting to fix my bad posture. The two Johns at Seaport Surveys for technical support. Bill Barry, Matt Barker, Stephanie Philbrick, Herb Adams, and all the other Portland history buffs who live in the past via dusty old texts and hard-to-read newspaper clippings. Ethan Minton for insight. Dave Noyes for great conversations. And to Bobby Reynolds for being my friend.

Much gratitude to the posse: Henry Wolyniec and J.T., Amy and Matt Kretz, Tanya Whiton and Paul Chamberlain, Liz Peavey and John McLoughlin, Lisa Whelan, Tanja Alexia Hollander, Darien Brahms and Leyli Johnson for keeping the decks clear.

A huge thanks to Patrick Corrigan, Clog Wornog, and Fuvvie (rhymes with lovey) for the most excellent illustrations and everything else.

And my endless gratitude and love to Shoshannah and Mabel, the ones responsible for making Portland the best place on the planet for me to live.

Yarmouth

Cumberland

Cousins I.

Littlejohn I.

Casco *Bay*

Great
Chebeague I.

Little
Chebeague I.

Cliff I.

Falmouth

Mackworth I.

Long I.

Jewell I.

Great
Diamond I.

Little
Diamond I.

Peaks I.

Portland

House I.

Cushing I.

So. Portland

PORTLAND UNDERCOVER

TABLE OF CONTENTS

INTRODUCTION

Here's a few things you need know about Portland, Maine

Portland has all the amenities of a major metropolis with the feel of a small town. Everything you need is located on an easily walkable three and a half-mile peninsula on the shores of Casco Bay providing unforgettable views of islands and ocean. A vibrant and modern city with a booming economy, Portland's waterfront is beautifully gritty and busy with fishing boats, freighters, tankers, and cruise ships. The neighborhoods are diverse with intricate and historic architecture. We have dozens of great restaurants and bars. The arts and music scene is eclectic and hip. The politics are fairly progressive and the weather is generally beautiful. Sure, we've got our problems, notably a shortage of low-income housing and a rising homeless population, but nothing like Boston or New York. Crime is low, with just a handful of murders annually. And unlike most cities, we don't have a "bad section" of town to avoid.

Some Mainers don't like visitors. Can you blame them? While merchants depend heavily on tourism, many locals resent the longer lines at stores and restaurants in the summer. Parking gets harder to find and the sandy beaches fill with out-of-staters. But don't let that stop you from visiting our fair city. As long as you have a copy of *Portland Undercover* hidden in a newspaper, no one will know you are "from away."

You need this guide because our peninsula is blessed with a refreshing shortage of franchise restaurants and stores. Here, you're faced with a unusual dilemma in modern American times: How to survive in a city filled with owner-operated shops and eateries. After reading *Portland Undercover*, you'll learn where to dine, drink, and explore without looking like a tourist. Unless, of course, you're too lazy to walk. Then we'll spot your foreign license plates and your cover is blown.

1

WHY YOU SHOULD VISIT PORTLAND

Here's a relaxing New England vacation: Spend an unhurried week in Portland, eat every meal at a different great restaurant, and leisurely discover our rich history, beautiful islands, unique shops and magnificent views. Head to the beach for a day with a pulp novel. Hop aboard a harbor cruise with a picnic lunch. Walk around the Arts District and check out the many galleries. Then enjoy a delicious dinner. Most of Maine goes to bed by 10 P.M., but in the big city we stay up until at least one in the morning. Go to the theater, the movies, or catch a hot local band or a national act with a Portland tour date. Play darts or shoot pool in one of the dozens of saloons in the cobblestoned Old Port. And when you see the moon casting silver light onto the islands and Casco Bay, you will be happy you came to Portland.

We have people

Portland is the state's cultural, business, and population center. Home to the state's top art museums and galleries, we have the largest symphony, the most accomplished theater and dance companies and Maine's only professional sports teams — Double A baseball's Portland Sea Dogs and the American Hockey League's Portland Pirates. The port is thriving, recently surpassing Boston in the handling of bulk cargo. More fish land here than anywhere else in New England. And in a state devoid of skyscrapers, the half-dozen bank-occupied high-rise buildings towering over Portland's downtown is the closest Maine has to a financial district. A handful of small colleges and two of Maine's largest hospitals are within the city limits. Although Augusta is the legislative capital, Portland is the state's center of law, home to the Supreme Court and more lawyers than necessary.

Almost a quarter of Maine's population, about 230,000 people, live in Greater Portland, with about 65,000 living in the city proper. Until 25 years ago Portland was very Caucasian, but thanks to the resettlement of political refugees from Vietnam, Cambodia, and several African countries, the community is now about 10 percent non-white. By Maine standards, that's quite diverse. And more transplants live in Portland than anywhere else in the state, giving the city an almost cosmopolitan flare. People-watching could be a full-time job, thanks to the random and lively mix of social classes in a relatively small population. Pierced hipsters sell coffee to the homeless and the bankers. Punk kids with fuchsia Mohawks sit on park benches next to muttering old men while Somali women in traditional dress wait for the bus. Fishermen reeking of rotten bait wait in line at sandwich shops behind stylish employees of Old Port boutiques. Bartenders take lunch orders from moneyed tourists oblivious to the jealous starving artist perched a couple of stools away, nursing cheap beer and anxiously awaiting happy hour.

We have at least four seasons

Portland's summers are fabulous. That's why most tourists come in June, July, and August. Daytime temps range generally between 70° and 80° F. Most days, shorts and T-shirts are all you need. Once a summer we experience a heat wave when the mercury hovers in the mid-90s for a week. But Yankee thrift prohibits spending money on rarely used appliances, so few buildings have air conditioning. The sea breeze kicks up mid-afternoon so if you're on or near the water, a windbreaker comes in handy. On some nights, a sweater and trousers will be appreciated. Always be prepared for rain, though the last few years have been abnormally dry. Even in the drizzle and fog, Portland is fun to explore. You'll just get a little wet. Be sure to make reservations ahead during the summer months; otherwise be prepared for a long hunt and possibly fruitless search for lodging.

Here's a little secret: Portland winters aren't as cold as you might expect. Due to the city's seaside location, temps generally range between 20° and 40° F from late November to March. Even so, the winter can be bone chilling and biting, so bring your warmest foul weather clothes. Spend a weekend here on your way north for a ski vacation. Most room rates are cut by at least 10 percent. You can always get a good table at the best restaurants. Bartenders are eager to please. The winter views of the harbor and bay are stunning, especially on freezing mornings when ice-covered fishing boats make their way into port surrounded by billowing sea smoke, the result of the collision between frigid air and warmer seawater.

After several months of winter, however, the locals grow weary of filthy snowbanks, the freezing temperatures and icy wind. That's why Mainers love spring. Also known as mud season, thanks to melting snow and frequent rains, the grass grows green once again, trees begin to bud and blossom and gardeners labor in their back-yard plots.

We have great sidewalks

Unlike most American cities these days, Portland's peninsula is completely walkable and meant to be explored on foot. Automobiles are unnecessary and while parking isn't impossible to find, it can be a hassle, so consider leaving your car at home. Fly into the International Jetport and take a taxi to your hotel. Or jump on a bus; most major lines service the city. And any year now, passenger rail service is expected to return.

But if you must drive, here's a tip: Avoid crossing the Maine-New Hampshire border on Fridays in the summer and don't try to leave the state on a Sunday or the Monday of a long holiday weekend. That way you'll miss the miles-long traffic jams at the entrance to the Maine turnpike. Once you make it past the toll plaza, it's a little less than 45 minutes to exit 6A and Route 295 into the city. Take Exit 4, follow the signs to the "Portland Waterfront" and you've arrived. Here you are greeted by piles of rusting steel, sparkling hills of crushed glass and huge tankers heavy with crude oil unloading at industrial wharves. Park the car where you're staying and spend the rest of your time in town as a pedestrian.

Here's a basic Portland geography lesson. Take a look at the map on page 78. Most places you want to visit are on the peninsula. To get your orientation, put the harbor to your right and Munjoy Hill rising out of the city in front of you; you're facing east. The main streets that run east to west are Commercial, Fore, Middle, Spring, Congress, and Cumberland Ave. The major streets run north and south, such as State, High, and Franklin Arterial. Motorists should be aware of Maine's strict drunk driving laws. State law requires you to always stop for pedestrians in crosswalks. But that shouldn't matter, since you don't want to drive. From the car you don't get to see the freaks wandering the streets or the bizarre sidewalk episodes that make life in Portland so interesting. Staying in the car means you'll miss the quirky little shops and architectural details that make Portland different in these times of global homogenization.

Why listen to me

I'm not a travel writer visiting Portland for the weekend relying on brochures handed out by the Chamber of Commerce to tell you about the good times to be had. I live here and love the city and never plan on leaving. For the last half dozen years I've worked as a print and radio journalist in Portland, occasionally posing undercover as a panhandler or homeless person to investigate issues from a perspective usually not found in the media. So I know these streets. Before moving to Portland, I spent two years lobstering on Matinicus, a remote Maine Island. And I served for three years as a sailor in the U.S. Coast Guard before that. So I know what it means to live on the ocean.

This is a portrait of a unique American city and a peninsula where Wal-Mart has yet to encroach. A place where artists flock because of the way the sunlight makes the remarkable architecture and landscape glow. A city of brick buildings and cobblestone alleys that smell of the ocean. A city populated with resourceful people who chose to live here because the quality of life is so damn great. Enjoy your stay.

2

AN ALTERNATIVE HISTORY

Portland wasn't always called Portland. For several millenniums, the natives hunted and gathered here each summer. This spot was a virgin peninsula of swamps, streams, beaches and rocky coast surrounded by a bay teeming with fish. They called the land Machigonne and the waters Aucocisco. When the white settlers arrived, they found the names too difficult to pronounce. So they called the bay "Casco" and the shores were called Falmouth. The peninsula became known as the "Neck" because it resembles a gullet. Thankfully, the townspeople wanted a new name and in 1786, they voted to call this place Portland. (For convenience sake, I will refer to the early settlement as Portland because "early Falmouth" is just too cumbersome and confusing. Today Falmouth is the high-priced suburb just north of Portland.)

Cheaters and wretches

Just like everywhere else in the New World, scoundrels and shysters stole this land from the indigenous people. An English servant named Walter Bagnall was the first European to permanently settle here. He came to Maine in 1628 after Massachusetts Puritans banned him from the colony for participating in swinging parties thrown by his boss. Before Bagnall, various explorers and fishermen visited the area, but he was the first to actually stay. Known as "Great Walt," he was an enormous man who set up shop on Richmond Island off Cape Elizabeth. He traded cheap goods to the Indians in exchange for beaver pelts. Bagnall resold the furs to Bostonians at an incredible markup. The natives knew they were being ripped off and weren't happy with the deal. And it didn't help that Great Walt was consorting with several local women. After three years of his shenanigans, the Indians had enough. They killed Bagnall and burned his buildings to the ground.

Despite his violent end, Great Walt had amassed a small fortune and proved there was money to be made on the shores of Casco Bay. Soon, more miscreants headed north to the wilderness in search of riches, including George Cleeve and Richard Tucker, the pair generally credited for settling the area. Other New Englanders viewed early Portland as a decadent territory filled with fornicators, adulterers and drunkards with bastard, unbaptized children. (More on this in Chapter 9.) If it wasn't for the abundance of convenient seafood, those early settlers would have certainly starved to death. They were too busy quarreling to plant enough crops. When they weren't cheating the Indians, they were bickering among themselves, oftentimes in Massachusetts courts, over who owned the land stolen from the natives. For almost 50 years, until the 1670s, Portland was without law or government. But as the population grew, greedy politicians in England and Massachusetts took notice and began scheming to take control of the region.

Legends on land and water

Whenever humans settle near the ocean, they tell tales about creatures lurking below the surface. William Willis, the preeminent local historian of the 19th century, retells an incident from back in 1639 when a birdhunter in a canoe was accosted by a merman, a male mermaid. The monster allegedly grabbed hold of the boat and spoke in a strange tongue. The hunter took his knife and hacked at this triton, slicing off an arm. And the beast sank to the depths, leaving the water purple with his blood.

I don't believe it. The creature was more likely a drowning Indian or Frenchman, but the hunter, probably drunk, didn't know any better. I do believe, however, the stories of sea serpents living in the area. Over the centuries, local sailors frequently reported sightings of large monsters near Casco Bay. Skeptics may laugh, but perhaps the elusive giant squid occasionally ventures into our waters.

Buried treasure is another popular marine myth. Several islands in Casco Bay are rumored to be the site of chests of gold hidden by pirates. Captain Kidd was said to have stashed valuables in a fresh-water pond on Jewell Island, but no one has admitted to finding them. On Great Chebeague Island, a one-eyed pirate reportedly put a hex on a young man who was following him during his search for stashed pieces of eight and gold doubloons. Within a year, the cursed lad died from painful cramps. Again, no claims of discovery.

The fourth time is a charm

In the almost four centuries since Portland was settled by the white man, the city has been destroyed four times. Twice during Indians wars, once by a British bombardment, and once by a massive fire that left thousands homeless. Luckily, the city's motto is *Resurgam*. (For the those not fluent in Latin, that means "we shall rise again.")

History books discuss King Philip's War, which began around 1675, as some of the bloodiest battles of America's colonial times. And since history is written by the winners, the Indians are usually portrayed as butchering savages. But try to look at it from their perspective. What would you do if a bunch of long-haired, foul-smelling, drunken, fornicating, immoral white folk came to your town, stole your property, had sex with your daughters and cheated you in every business transaction? Most people, I think, would try to get rid of the troublemakers.

That's what happened in 1676. Back then, about 40 families of settlers were living in Portland. The natives, frustrated by the behavior of these new residents, raided the town, killing as many white people as possible. (Other Indian tribes staged similar assaults at the same time further south on the Maine coast.) The surviving townspeople hid on Cushing Island until armed Massachusetts soldiers arrived and escorted the frightened inhabitants to safety. For a couple of years, the settlement was deserted.

In 1678, the warring parties signed a truce. Portland was resettled and each family was required to give the natives one peck of corn annually for rent. But the Massachusetts government didn't trust the Indians, so Fort Loyal was built in the area now known as India Street in case of future attacks. The white folk didn't learn their lesson and continued to cheat the natives whenever they could. Ten years after the resettlement, the town's population swelled to about 600. Then the French and Indian wars began.

One possible slaughter was avoided in 1689 because a squadron of Indian fighters arrived the day before a battle on the Brackett family farm now called Deering Oaks. It was a bloody six-hour brawl that left 10 white soldiers dead and another dozen seriously injured. But the Indians and the French retreated. The soldiers hung around for a month, then departed, despite the settlers' fears of another attack.

The next spring, the French and the Indians prepared for one more offensive. They ambushed a group of soldiers on Munjoy Hill, killing 13. The locals scrambled for refuge in Fort Loyal. Once all the settlers were inside the garrison, the almost 500 attackers burned the rest of the settlement to the ground. For five days, the fort was besieged. Finally, with food and ammo running low, the fort's commander asked for a truce. The French and the Indians agreed. The massive doors were opened and the Indians stormed the fort, killing and scalping everyone but five soldiers who were captured and taken to Canada. And for the next 26 years, early Portland was abandoned.

By 1718, settlers began to return without fear of Indian attacks since most of the trouble-making tribes had been eliminated. (I'm embarrassed to tell you that until 1954, Native Americans didn't have the right to vote in Maine.) For most of the 17th century the town prospered and grew, eventually becoming home to almost 2,000 inhabitants. The most lucrative industry of the times was the mast trade. Maine's tall white pines were used by the British navy for spars aboard their warships. (England was running out of trees, but the colonies were green with lumber.) Fur and fish also generated profit for Portland. In those pre-Revolutionary times, however, hatred for the British rule and taxes was growing. Angry locals began harassing the King's Loyalists, eventually capturing English naval officer Captain Henry Mowat and two other Tories. After a couple of days, the trio was released unharmed. Unfortunately for Portlanders, Mowat didn't forget his abduction.

On October 18, 1775, Mowat returned to Casco Bay, accompanied by a squadron of naval warships and desire for revenge. Under orders to destroy the town, he was happy to oblige. He gave the settlement a couple hours' warning to remove women and children to safety. Then his ships unleashed a bombardment of massive proportions. For five hours cannonballs and bombs rained down and the town became engulfed in flames. But Mowat was not satisfied. He sent a landing party ashore to ensure the job was finished. His men proceeded to set fire to most of the structures still standing. Interestingly, Mowat's fury saved other rebelling ports from a similar fate. The silly Englishman used all his ammo during the bombardment. The destruction of Portland is referred to — however obliquely — in the Declaration of Independence. In the list of the King's transgressions against the colonies, he is blamed for having plundered "our Sea, ravaged our coasts, burnt our towns and destroyed the lives of our people."

A Fiery Fourth

Again, Portlanders worked together to rise from the ashes. Modern buildings were constructed on Fore, India, and what is now Congress Street. For the next several decades, Portland's economy prospered, then faltered, then prospered once more. The details are boring, but in 1820 Maine became a state, finally free from Massachusetts. The rich made and lost fortunes while the poor struggled endlessly against the oppressive beast of a new Republic dominated by patriarchal, slave-owning white men. And booze became illegal. (Read Chapter 5). Then disaster struck once more.

On the afternoon of July 4, 1866, a young boy celebrating Independence Day tossed a firecracker into a barrel of wood shavings at a boatyard on Commercial Street near High Street. A building was soon ablaze, but the fire brigade arrived and put out the flames. The heroes congratulated themselves and left, not knowing the afternoon breeze had carried hot cinders to the roof of the nearby Portland Sugar House. Soon the factory, where molasses was made into sugar and syrups, and a couple of neighboring foundries were engulfed in flames. The blaze spread quickly, fanned by increasingly stronger winds. It didn't help that the tide was out, so firefighters couldn't pump seawater to battle the growing inferno. And the brigade from the nearby Brackett Street firehouse was not available. They were 15 miles away at Sebago Lake for their annual Fourth of July picnic.

When the fire eventually burned itself out on a sandy stretch of Munjoy Hill, an astonishing one-third of the city was gone. More than 1,500 buildings were leveled by flames. Historian Edward Elwell described the downtown as a "wilderness of chimneys." Ten thousand people were left homeless. Amazingly, only two people were killed.

More than $10 million in damages were reported. In addition to residential housing, City Hall, eight churches, six hotels, and all the banks and newspapers were destroyed. Donations poured in from around the world as international media reported the devastation. Once again, Portlanders rebuilt from ashes. Tent cities were set up atop Munjoy Hill and slowly the reconstruction began. It wasn't easy. Heavy snowstorms hit the city later that year in the midst of rebuilding.

Ironically, the fire was a blessing for the city. Portland became a modern place, with all the latest conveniences and technology. New laws prohibited the construction of wooden buildings in the business district. While many of the facades of the Old Port buildings may appear to be carved wood, they're actually cast iron. Crooked footpaths were straightened and widened into streets. A water pipeline from Sebago Lake to the city was constructed and Lincoln Park was built as a firebreak between downtown and the new residential neighborhoods.

A suicidal outlaw

In the early 1800s, Portland was a tiny hamlet with just 3,000 inhabitants, mostly living near the harbor. But it was dangerous place. Unscrupulous sea captains shanghaied unsuspecting sailors who would then awaken miles out to sea enroute to foreign lands. Back on shore, heavy-drinking thugs roamed the waterfront, ready to slice a man's throat at the first sight of gold. Who knows how many murder victims were unceremoniously dumped into the ocean?

Herbert Jones tells a good crime story in his hard-to-find 1938 book, *Old Portland Town*. One August morning in 1818, the cashier of the local bank discovered the vault completely cleaned out. More than $200,000 was missing, a huge fortune in those days. The police believed the crooks were still in town. They suspected a man named George Manley and a shady confederate named Rolfe. Investigators interrogated Rolfe first. He broke under pressure and confessed to helping Manley. He offered to bring the cops to the place where they stashed the loot. Rolfe lead the constables to a waterfront location near India Street. By candlelight the police shoveled and shoveled. But the money had disappeared. Rolfe realized he was in trouble. Somehow he grabbed a gun and shot himself in a head, his corpse tumbling into a ready grave, the hole the officers had dug.

The authorities then paid Manley a visit, informing him of Rolfe's confession. (They neglected to mention his suicide.) Manley was offered a deal: A dozen years behind bars and part of the reward offered by the bank for the return of the money. He accepted the plea bargain and brought the police out to the Scarborough Marsh. Manley hadn't trusted Rolfe, so he had rehidden the loot in the clam flats. But he couldn't find the cash. Turns out two locals spotted a strange man stashing something in the marsh. They went and recovered the money, returning it to the law. After his stint in prison, Manley came back to Portland, Jones wrote, and went into business using the reward as seed money. Apparently he was a law-abiding citizen until his death. Manley is buried in the Eastern Cemetery, the city's oldest, on the foot of Munjoy Hill.

Teach a man to fish and he'll deplete an ocean

Many early Portland residents made their living as seamen, and, without weather forecasts and high-tech navigation equipment, they were at the mercy of storms and wooden boats. Many widows waited for years, not knowing if their husbands were dead or alive. News traveled back slowly then and vessels often went down without a trace or whisper. But there was money to be made, so for many the risk was necessary.

While the lobster is heavily identified today with Maine, 150 years ago fishermen ignored tasty seabugs. Since the *homarus americanus* should be killed just prior to eating, it couldn't be shipped. Back then, the crustacean was so plentiful that prison inmates, the indigent elderly, and orphans were fed lobster regularly. Farmers used lobsters to fertilize the land. But with the invention of the canning process, lobsters suddenly became valuable. (Canned lobster? Yuck!) With eventual improvements in transportation, lobsters were shipped alive. In 1998, over $137 million dollars worth of lobsters were caught in the waters off Maine.

Unfortunately, fishermen are greedy. They have to be. Most are honest and hardworking, but it's their job to catch as many fish as possible. Thanks to new gear and better, faster boats — the Gulf of Maine fish stocks are rapidly depleting. The government only recently stepped up conservation measures via shorter seasons, stricter quotas, and temporary closings of fishing areas. Fishermen — most of those involved in the industry are male — loudly complain about the meddling regulators.

Who knows if the strict new rules will be enough to replenish the fish stocks? There is a glimmer of hope. A couple years back, before the dredging of Portland Harbor, fishermen and environmentalists worked together in a "lobster relocation program." They caught and moved tens of thousands of undersized lobsters to a location outside the harbor before the massive cranes could crush the small lobsters while scooping tons of silt from the shipping channel. Other similar cooperative efforts between government, environmentalists and fisherman will be necessary to save the industry.

3

ACCOMMODATIONS

I t is very important to make reservations for lodging before you plan a summer trip to Portland, otherwise you may find yourself sleeping in the car. While there are thousands of rooms in the region, most are booked weeks, if not months, in advance. What follows are brief descriptions of eight unique hotels and B&Bs located on the peninsula. (All have free parking, unless otherwise noted.) I've included contact numbers for other establishments. I also provide a couple locations for snoozing when you can't find a bed. Exact room prices are not included because many innkeepers still haven't set the rates for the summer. **(Note: Maine has one telephone area code: 207.)**

The Danforth, 163 Danforth Street, 879-8755

Built in 1821, this West End inn was tastefully restored several years ago after years of neglect and a fire. While original architecture is from the Federal period, the cupola where you are welcome to watch the sunrise and sunset, is of Italianate style. Rates range from $169 to $299. The most expensive room is actually a grand suite with a queen-size foldout couch in the second room and a private deck that looks over the neighborhood.

Eastland Park Hotel, 157 High Street, 775-5411

When the hotel opened in 1927, the original owners made a big deal of dropping the front door keys from an airplane into the harbor, boasting that the Eastland would never close. Let's hope so. The views from the upper floors are fabulous, so ask for a room looking toward the ocean. Parking is available nearby for $6.50 daily.

Inn on Carleton, 46 Carleton Street, 775-1910

Not only is this West End B&B the longest running in Portland, it is also the most beautiful. Built in 1869, the ceilings are over ten feet high. The wood floors are stunning and the furnishings, mostly huge Victorian antiques, are better than you would ever expect to find in a B&B. Be sure to examine the trompe l'oeil artwork in the foyer by Charles Schumacher. Recently restored to its original beauty, the painting reminds you how much time and effort went into building and decorating these grand old homes. Rates range between $140 and $200 and you will not be disappointed.

Inn at Park and Spring, 135 Spring Street, 774-1059

This B&B is just a couple minutes walk from the Portland Museum of Art and several tasty restaurants. The first floor of the inn is charming with floor to ceiling windows, beautifully restored hardwood floors, exquisite crystal chandeliers and a great color scheme. The rates are reasonable, between $130 and $145, and a two-night stay is required on summer weekends.

Inn at St. John, 939 Congress Street, 773-6481

This 100-year-old hotel is the best deal in town for lodging with rates ranging from $54 to $140. Five years ago, this was rundown and almost a flophouse. Today, it's dog-friendly, clean, and quaint, with an almost European feel. While the hotel is a short stroll to Thai food and Hadlock Field, home to the Portland Sea Dogs baseball team — it takes about 20 minutes to walk to downtown and the Old Port. But since you save at least 50 bucks a night staying here, the walk is well worth it.

Oak Leaf Inn, 51A Oak Street, 773-7882

This downtown hotel is another property that once suffered from years of neglect. But the new owners are in the process of renovation, room by room. The prices are reasonable, between $90 and $190, but you feel like you're stuck in the 1950s. Be sure to request a room with a view and you'll wake to stunning sunrises. The Oak Leaf is very convenient to everything on the peninsula.

The Portland Regency Hotel, 20 Milk Street, 774-4200

The best thing about this Old Port hotel is the brick exterior. Built at the end of the 19th century, originally this was the State of Maine Armory. While some of the more expensive suites are very nice, the low ceilings and carpet in the cheaper rooms feel like a Holiday Inn. For $200 a night, you're basically paying for the convenience of being in the Old Port. Valet parking is $8 a day.

Victorian Terrace, 84 Eastern Promenade, 774-9083

You won't find any rooms in Portland with more sweeping panoramas than at the Victorian Terrace. Part B&B and part short-term apartment rentals, this is the only lodging in the East End and the only one in the city with weekly rates. The Terrace is actually three neighboring large buildings on the end of the Prom near Fore Street. Every room is nonsmoking and has a view of Casco Bay and the islands. You're paying for the views, so the rates ($110 to $250) are a little on the high side for the facilities, but it's worth it. The Old Port and downtown are a 20-minute walk away. (The trip back takes longer because you're climbing Munjoy Hill.)

Other Local Lodging Options

Anchor Motel, 715 Main Street, South Portland 775-9011

Andrews B&B, 417 Auburn Street, 797-9157

Chadwick B&B, 140 Chadwick Street, 774-5141

Downeaster Motel, Route One, Scarborough, 883-6004

Inn By the Sea, 40 Bowery Road, Cape Elizabeth, 799-3134, (very dog friendly)

Maine Motel, 606 Main Street South Portland, 774-8284

Moosehead Motel, Route One Scarborough, 883-4422

Parkside Parrot, 273 State Street, 775-0224

Percy Inn, 15 Pine Street, 871-7638

Pine Haven Motel, 857 Main Street, South Portland, 772-4057

Pomegranate Inn, 49 Neal Street, 772-1006

Pride Motel, Route One, Scarborough, 883-4816

West End Inn, 146 Pine Street, 772-1377

If you can't find a room

A buddy of mine once spent a whole summer sleeping in his car on the Eastern Prom. The view was great and so was the rent. I've known others who parked on Commercial Street for some uninterrupted late night slumber. I checked with a highly placed Portland police source and he says that in most cases, if lodging truly isn't available, the police officer will more than likely allow you to catch some shut-eye, just as long you're not misbehaving in a vehicle. The more adventuresome could try their luck in Hobo Village, a wooded area near the industrial waterfront, where blue tarps and tents are home to a couple of wanderers. Just be careful.

4

FOOD

Some like to brag that Portland is second only to San Francisco in number of restaurants per capita. I can't verify the data and who cares anyway? Just walk the streets of the Old Port around suppertime and your nose will be inundated with more tantalizing aromas than you can identify. Trivial dining statistics won't matter any longer.

Wine and beer connoisseurs will be happy in Portland. Maine microbrews are well-known for being among the best in America. Shipyard, Geary's, Allagash, Sea Dog, Bray's, and Carrabassett are all dependable brands. And most of the restaurants I've recommended for dinner have great and varied wine lists. Vino drinkers should know that under state law, you can bring an unfinished bottle home with you. (Unfortunately, the law doesn't cover beer.) The restaurant can deny the privilege if for some reason management thinks it's a bad idea. (Like you just bragged about being able to drink the bottle in the car while driving home.) Remember, Maine has tough drunk driving laws. You should expect a trip to the Cumberland County Jail if pulled over with a .08 blood alcohol percentage.

Anyone who enjoys a good cup of joe will love Portland's locally owned coffee shops. The following are highly recommended: Arabica (16 Free Street), any of the three Coffee By Design locations, Java Joe's on lower Exchange Street and at the Public Market, Portland Coffee Roasters (111 Commercial).

While visiting our fair city, take a moment to think about the people who serve you in the fabulous restaurants. Friends who wait tables roll their eyes when I ask about tourists. Many are generous, they say, but the cheapskates make the job tough. Remember, you're supporting the arts. Very few servers are merely waitrons. Most have other gigs as poets, painters, filmmakers, sculptors, or musicians.

If you're a smoker, be aware that all of Maine's restaurants are smoke-free. The only exceptions are "lounges" (some lounges serve food) where people under 21 aren't allowed without a parent.

This chapter is not an all-inclusive listing of restaurants in Portland. What's the point in telling you about bad food or tourists traps? While some restaurants omitted from this chapter are worth exploring, I've provided more than enough options to survive a week in the city without visiting the same place twice. These are in a very rough order of preference from high end to casual to lunch, then breakfast.

First, a word about lobsters

Portlanders usually don't order lobsters in restaurants because you can save around ten bucks a person by dropping the lobster in a pot of boiling water yourself. Besides, lobsters are best eaten at a friend's camp (that's what Mainers call cottages) or at a island lobster feed with cold beer and laughter. Most of the restaurants included here generally don't serve the traditional steamed lobster dinner. If that's what you want, try J's Oyster, Gilbert's, or Newick's (just over the bridge in South Portland.)

Katahdin, 106 High Street, 774-1740

Katahdin will always hover at the top of my list. After dozens of visits, I've never had a bad meal here. The martinis by Michelle are out of this world and the largest in Portland, be sure to ask for the jalapeno olives. (One martini equals two and half elsewhere. The overfill is kept cold in a beaker on ice.) Everything on the menu is delicious, especially the soups, the mesclun salads, Linda's Crab Dip, the pot roast, and all the seafood. The desserts are homemade and decadent. The servers are well informed and funny. Definitely worth the wait if there's a line.

Local 188, 188 State Street, 761-7909

Reluctantly, I'm telling you about Local 188. I'd rather be selfish and keep this great tapas bar and gallery a secret, but it wouldn't be fair to fans of Spanish-influenced food and cutting edge, eclectic art. Other Portland restaurants hang paintings on the walls, but here art is just as important as the food. And the food is terrific. Run by a collective of talented artists, including *Portland Undercover* illustrator Pat Corrigan, Local became an instant hotspot with hipsters since opening in the spring of 1999. The shrimp, clams, and mussels are all tasty here, often served with chorizo sausage, and with an unbelievable broth perfect for dipping the Standard Bakery baguettes. Since Local is a tapas bar, portions are intentionally on the small side. Create your own private smorgasbord to share among the members of your party. Local has beer and wine, with a good, though limited, selection of Spanish rioja wines. Sunday brunch is one of the best in Portland.

Café Uffa, 190 State Street, 775-3380

Sometimes you may have to wait a half-hour for a table at Café Uffa because the people inside just don't want to leave. The food and staff are great and the restaurant is beautiful, with high ceilings, wooden booths, and interesting art. The huge front window gives most diners a broad view of the back of Longfellow's statue. Uffa's wine list is extensive and any salad is guaranteed to please. For many years, Uffa primarily offered delicious vegetarian and seafood entrees, but recently added a mouth-watering rib-eye steak to the menu. Brunch on Saturday and Sunday is packed with hipsters recovering from the night before with help from coffee, and animated conversation. And Uffa is perhaps the only high-end restaurant in Portland with a round table large enough to seat eight.

Street and Company, 33 Wharf Street, 775-0887

This seafood restaurant has a very European feel, especially on summer nights if you're lucky enough to be dining outside on the cobblestoned street. A large window on the kitchen allows you to watch the chefs juggle sizzling pans filled with flames. My favorite is the clams and pasta. The menu is scrawled on portable chalkboards and the server grabs a nearby chair for an easel.

Fore Street, 288 Fore Street, 775-2717

You're going to spend some cash here, but it's worth it. Dana Street's second restaurant, grander than Street and Company, was instantly popular with foodies when it opened a couple of years ago. The bar is elegant and hip with a fabulous wine list and the dining room is probably the most architecturally stunning in Portland. It used to be a furniture store, and before that a warehouse, at one point reportedly storing surplus tanks and artillery. The gigantic open kitchen is the centerpiece of the restaurant where a bustling staff of cooks work magic on meats, game and fowl over flaming grills and turnspits fired with apple wood. Be sure to order mussels if they're on the bill of fare. The hanger steak is also mouth-watering. Vegetarians have a few options here, but Fore Street is more for carnivores.

Perfetto, 28 Exchange Street, 828-0001

This colorful Mediterranean-influenced upscale Old Port restaurant is great for lunch and dinner. The bar is also popular because of the extensive wine list and high-end liquors. The portions are huge and the salads are tasty, especially the Caesar. (Be warned, this salad is for garlic-lovers only.) The salmon is always satisfying, either grilled or pan-seared, but the best entrée is probably the North Beach Cioppino, a local seafood served on pasta with a spicy lobster-stock marinara. For lunch, try the potpie, filled with a rustic stew and served in a very flaky crust.

Walter's, 15 Exchange Street, 871-9258

Walter's "New American" cuisine is popular with older foodies and younger hip gourmands. If lobster ravioli is on the bill of fare, treat yourself to an order. Pan-seared and delicious, this is one of the best ways to enjoy Maine's most famous crustacean. The lunchtime blue-plate special changes daily, is usually a bargain, and is always worth trying.

Bella Cucina, 653 Congress Street, 828-4033

Bella Cucina, another in a long line of restaurants involving famed chef Jim Leduc, calls its cuisine "Italian Inspired." No spaghetti and meatballs here, but for discerning palates, there's an entrée for every taste. The menu changes daily, but always includes vegan, veggie, seafood and wood-grilled meats entrees. Excellent wine list and desserts.

Benkay, 2 India Street, 773-5555

Of the three sushi bars on the peninsula, Benkay is the most authentic. A friend who once lived in Japan says Benkay's sushi is the highest quality and freshest in the city. And she says Benkay follows closely to the traditional ways of sushi restaurants by frequently showing sumo wrestling and other Japanese TV shows on the television.

Ribollita, 41 Middle Street, 774-2972

Locals love the taste of the semi-rustic Tuscan cuisine and the generous portions. Try the roasted eggplant filled with spinach and ricotta served over pasta, or anything on the menu featuring chicken livers. The mussels and the onion tart are also recommended. For dinner on Friday or Saturday night, call at least three or four days ahead for reservations.

Norm's BBQ, 43 Middle Street, 774-6711

I've never had the fried chicken at Norm's BBQ because it takes 30 minutes to fry and you can't call ahead to start the process. I'm sure it's good though, because the chicken is fresh, not frozen, and prepared to order. Norm and his ragamuffin staff of chefs know how to cook. This is gourmet barbecue with the strong taste and smell of down-home backyard pits. The sauces are zesty and ribs are cooked tender to the bone. It's difficult to decide what to have at

Norms, but I highly recommend the steak tips and the BBQ chicken. Beer and wine only here, and you'll probably end up sharing a table with strangers since seating is community style.

Norm's Bar and Grill, 606 Congress Street, 828-9944

Norm calls his second establishment a tapas bar, but that's stretching it a bit. Another hot spot with the hipsters, especially before and after concerts at the State Theater, the food could be called elevated pub fare. The burgers are good, as is the BBQ chicken quesadilla and the black bean soup is among the tastiest in Portland. Consider yourself blessed if you get the window booth, one of the most sought after tables in the city.

Uncle Billy's BBQ, 69 Newbury Street, 871-5631

Uncle Billy's is in an unusual location, but everything about owner Jonathan St. Laurent is a bit strange. My choice for the city's funkiest restaurant, the waiters are a little crazy and the décor is white-trash hill-billy chic. But the BBQ is outstanding. St. Laurent probably never met a pig he couldn't cook and the collard greens taste of the South. Be sure to play some old-time favorites on the jukebox.

Barbecue Bob's, 147 Cumberland Avenue 871-8894

Bob's is the most informal of Portland's barbeques, with dinner served on paper plates. But who cares about dishes when the ribs are this good? Sloppier meals are served on a bed of white bread on the paper plates to absorb the extra sauce. Bob's only problem is the lack of table space during the dinner rush, but a moonlit barbecue picnic on the nearby (eight blocks uphill) Eastern Promenade is a lovely way to spend an evening.

Granny's Burritos, 420 Fore Street, 761-0751

Granny's started as a small burrito stand in the mid 1990s and now is one of Portland's most popular and healthy restaurants. The menu is limited to burritos, quesadillas, and nachos, but all items are available in vegan, veggie, chicken, and beef formats. Out of an unbelievable selection of tortillas, I recommend the sun-dried tomato or the spinach. One burrito is enough to satisfy the hungriest explorer. Downstairs is casual with picnic tables, upstairs is casual with beer and wine and occasional live music.

Federal Spice, 225 Federal Street, 774-6404

Open for lunch and dinner, Federal Spice is another great spot for upscale wraps and quesadillas. Owner Steve Johnson comes up with tasty specials with fish and fowl influenced by Caribbean, Italian, and Spanish cuisine. The wraps are high-end but affordable, usually around six bucks. The yam fries and the spicy french fries are both quite popular with the locals. And during the summer, the patio along the Federal Street sidewalk is the place to sit and watch legal types scurry to the courthouse.

Mexican food

Portland really needs a good Mexican restaurant. While many lefties (as in politics) enjoy Mesa Verde on Congress Street because of the wholesome and organic foods, this isn't traditional Mexican fare. Margaritas on Brown Street is popular with yuppie types, but I can't get over the orange cheese, the bright lights, stuffed piñatas and oversized sombreros. Amigos on Dana Street in the Old Port is known more for the bar downstairs than the dining, though the food is passable.

Seng Thai, 921 Congress Street, 879-2577
Seng Thai Restaurant, 265 St. John Street, 774-1959

If you can over the fluorescent lights, then both these restaurants are good for Thai food. The Congress Street eatery has long been a favorite for fast takeout. The pad Thai and spring rolls are very popular and are a good value for the price.

Vientiane Eat In and Take Out, 157 Noyes Street, 879-1614

Located in a suburban neighborhood near the University of South Maine just off the peninsula, Vientiane is about a half-hour walk from downtown, about 15 minutes from Deering Oaks. Both a restaurant and Thai grocery store, it's fun to browse among the shelves while waiting for your order.

Silly's, 40 Washington Avenue, 772-0360

It's the thriving home of the Abdullah, a roll-up with your choice of veggie, pulled pork, tuna, chicken, or deep fried haddock. The pizzas are delicious and so is anything with the Jamaican jerk chicken. The chocolate shakes and french fries are among the best in the city. If it's a nice night, eat outside in the kitschy backyard dining area lit by party lights and candles, but watch out for the bloodsucking mosquitoes.

Rosie's, 330 Fore Street, 772-5656
Ruski's, 212 Danforth Street, 774-7604

Steve and Rosie Harris own both Rosie's and Ruski's. Here's a little secret. These taverns have almost identical menus, but the prices at Rosie's in the high-rent Old Port are a buck and half more expensive. Ruski's, located in a working class neighborhood on the south side of the West End, is out-of-the-way, smaller and doesn't have as much seafood. Both are pubs with a serious devotion to darts and their curious mix of regulars. Smoking is encouraged here. Steve Harris is a loud guy, to put it mildly, and was a vocal opponent to the smoking ban. The Harrises are also extremely generous to charity, raising tens of thousands of dollars through benefits staged at the bars.

As for food, my favorites are the veggie burgers and the fried chicken dinner, but the hamburgers and chicken sandwiches are also quite tasty. Don't expect much from the salads, however. The calzones are bigger than your head and daily specials at Ruski's sometimes feature comfort foods like macaroni and cheese with a hotdog or a turkey dinner with all the fixings. The specials at Rosie's are a little more exotic, with peculiar animals. One recent offering included ostrich burgers. The beer list is better at Rosie's, but a couple good microbrews are available at Ruski's. And Ruski's opens for breakfast at seven in the morning, so don't be surprised by gangs of fishermen just returning from a couple weeks at sea and their pockets full of cash ordering beer and shots of whiskey with their steak and eggs.

Giobbi's, 1 Danforth Street, 772-0873

You won't find better pizza on the Portland peninsula. Located in Gorham's corner, near the statue dedicated to famous film director John Ford, Giobbi's is a family-style Italian restaurant with extremely reasonable prices. The traditional spaghetti and meatballs is a good value with hefty portions. But if you're in the mood for pizza, try a pie with ricotta, tomatoes, spinach and fresh garlic. The deep-fried raviolis are so good it's easy to forget what they must be doing to your cholesterol levels. On warm summer nights, the patio outside is great place for dinner and to people-watch.

The Italian sandwich

Back at the beginning of the 20th century, Giovanni Amato came from Italy to Portland via Brooklyn and eventually opened a bakery and store on India Street. Amato is generally credited with inventing the "Italian" sandwich made with salami and provolone on a white bread roll with olive oil. Nowadays, just about every convenience store sells and makes Italians. Over the years, the star of the sandwich became ham, though most places are more than willing to make an Italian with other meats or even all-veggie. Just to be safe, before ordering, ask what they put in the sandwich. Greek olives over black olives is usually a good sign.

Anthony's Italian Kitchen, 151 Middle Street, 774-8668

A favorite of Old Port office workers, Anthony's Italian Kitchen is especially busy during lunch hour dishing out spaghetti, linguini, ziti, and various other pasta dishes. Good slices for good prices and the pizza chefs pride themselves for going months without repeating a daily special. Lovers of high-end cold cuts should have the Boston Italian, filled with all sorts of salamis and hams. Several other sandwiches are worth sampling.

West End Grocery, 133 Spring Street, 874-6426

Part neighborhood store, part gourmet sandwich shop, all the ingredients used at the West End's are fresh and wholesome. Try the Caesar salad roll-up with chicken or the portabello mushroom and spinach roll-up. Equally delicious is the hearty meatloaf sandwich or the fresh mozzarella sandwich. The West End also sells hot prepared meals like roasted chicken or lasagna, at a good price, for take out. And the grocery section is well stocked.

Speciality vendors

Perry's Kosher Grill, corner of Commercial and Moulton streets

You can't miss Perry while walking along Commercial Street on a summer day. He's the guy blowing the shofar, a traditional Jewish ram's horn, in exchange for a donation to his favorite deserving charity. Try the hot dog and knish special, but be sure to let the doughy potatoes cool down for a minute or two before eating.

Mark's Hot Dogs corner of Exchange and Middle streets

Thankfully, one of the nicest people you'll meet in the Old Port is sturdy enough to stay open year round. The frankfurters here are standard, but a hot dog is merely a vehicle for condiments anyway. Chili, cheese, kraut, onions, ketchup, or mustard, Mark will hook you up. Location is key with a hot dog lunch. Both Tommy's Park and Post Office Park are mere footsteps away, so you won't have to hunt for a place to sit and eat.

Ice Cream

Some say ice cream was "invented" in Portland in 1825 by a man name David Robinson. Reportedly he made a flavored dairy concoction involving snow as a special treat for the Marquis de Lafayette. The tradition continues today.

Q's Ice Cream, 505 Fore Street, 773-7017

The ice cream is made on the premises in many flavors from very wholesome ingredients. You won't find chemical preservatives or artificial colors here. That's why the workers are always cheerful. Enjoy a cone or try a sundae, a frappe, or a brownie sandwich.

Beal's Old Fashioned Ice Cream Frozen Yogurt, 12 Moulton Street, 828-1335

Located smack dab in the middle of the Old Port, Beal's is part of tiny, locally owned family chain. Choose from over 60 flavors including some interesting twists on old standards. Unfortunately, Beal's is open only during the summer and early fall.

Ben and Jerry's, 425 Fore Street, 773-3222

The Exchange Street location opened in 1983 and is the oldest franchise outside Vermont. Ben and Jerry — the pair of hippies who changed the way humanity looks at ice cream — have long-time ties to Portland. Legend has it that Jerry got married here and one of their first teams of lawyers had an office upstairs on Exchange Street. Ironically, the price of a factory-packed pint of ice cream is about fifty cents more than the same pint at many local convenience stores.

Red's Dairy Freeze, 167 Cottage Road, South Portland. 799-7506

Everyone loves Red's, especially those who crave authentic soft serve in various flavors and toppings. The location along a fairly busy road and the lack of seating make for funny scenes. Red's usually opens by Saint Patrick's Day and closes sometime in October.

Kettle Cove Take-out and Dairy Bar, Route 77, Cape Elizabeth, 799-3533

Just beyond Two Lights State Park, this seasonal ice cream stand specializes in hard pack ice cream. I've stood in line for more than

20 minutes to get a cone, but it was worth the wait. If pumpkin ice cream is on the menu, order it. I was pleasantly surprised. And for a sly joke, be sure to ask for a bumper sticker.

Breakfast

In addition to the following breakfast joints, three restaurants mentioned above also offer breakfast. Café Uffa on Wednesday through Sunday, Local 188 for Sunday brunch, and don't forget Ruski's in the West End opens every morning at seven (Sundays at nine).

Becky's, 390 Commercial Street, 773-7070

Opening at 4 A.M., Becky's is popular with fishermen and stock-brokers alike. On weekend mornings the place is packed. The fruit bowl with yogurt and granola is surprisingly popular here, along with more traditional breakfast fare. Breakfast is served until four in the afternoon, just in case you get a late start on the day.

Marcy's, 47 Oak Street, 774-9713

Opening at 6 A.M., Marcy's, downstairs from the Oak Leaf Inn, is popular with downtown residents and alternative retro types. This is your standard greasy spoon, complete with a friendly wait-staff who treat the regulars like family, trading insults and jokes. When the diner is crowded, eating is a delicate affair, especially when the person sitting next to you weighs over 200 pounds.

Porthole, 20 Custom House Wharf, 761-7634

Located on a somewhat crumbling wharf, the Porthole offers standard diner fare at decent prices. The restaurant is clean and the food is tasty. For a good time, spend a leisurely morning with a newspaper or book on the Porthole's deck. Watch the gulls squab-ble over scraps of fish while you enjoy eggs, toast, and homefries.

Friendship Café, 703 Congress Street, 871-5005

Friendship Café is one of the healthier breakfast joints in the city. Choose from buckwheat pancakes, porridge, and fresh baked goods. Don't worry, eggs and bacon are also available. Friendship is especially refreshing during the annual weeklong summer heat wave, since the café is one of the rare Portland eateries with air conditioning.

Bagels

Alas, Portland is not perfect. Sure we have delicious food, incredible views, fascinating people and beautiful summers. However, we don't have decent bagels. Our local bagels aren't chewy or big enough and don't have the flavor of their cousins from New York City. That said, slop enough veggie cream cheese on a Portland bagel and you have breakfast. Mr. Bagel has two locations on the peninsula, 10 Moulton Street in the Old Port and at 539 Congress Street downtown. Bagelworks, at 15 Temple Street, is also popular with the natives.

Picnics

Portlanders love to eat outdoors, especially during nice weather. When you spend a quarter of the year wearing bulky sweaters and shivering in the icy winter wind, you take advantage of every beautiful warm summer day.

Portland Greengrocer, 211 Commercial Street, 761-9232

No one else in the city even comes close to the Greengrocer in terms of fruits and veggies. Year-round, the produce is good and fresh and the store is bright and cheery. Not only does the Greengrocer carry the city's best vegetables, you won't find better fresh chicken sausages anywhere. The store also stocks a fine selection of vinegar, oils, mustards, and nuts. The cheese selection is excellent and the wines are fabulous and fairly priced. Look for the signs proclaiming "good and cheap" wines. Owners John and Nick know a lot about food and love to talk about it, so feel free to pester them with questions.

Micucci's, 45 India Street, 775-1854

The area around India Street is known as Portland's Little Italy. The original Amato's, the alleged birthplace of the Italian sandwich, was here. The Village Café is nearby and so is St. Joseph's Roman Catholic Church. Many Italian families live in the neighborhood. But Micucci's puts the Italy in Little Italy. An excellent deli for cold cuts and Italian meats, this is where Portlanders with demanding tastes buy their mozzarella and parmesan. The wine and pasta are at bargains prices, maybe because the store is just a small part of a multi-million dollar family wholesale business that supplies Italian products to restaurants throughout northern New England.

PERFECT
PICNIC SPOTS

Eastern Promenade

Western Promenade

Deering Oaks Park

Tommy's Park

Post Office Park

Lincoln Park

Garden behind Longfellow House

First Parish Garden

Monument Square

Congress Square

Long Wharf

Maine State Pier

The Standard Baking Company, 75 Commercial Street, 773-2112

This is possibly the best bread in America. I can't imagine better bread. Baked on the premises, the loaves, the baguettes, rolls and sticky buns are always perfect. Standard is owned by Dana Street, the genius behind Street & Company and Fore Street restaurants. Until a couple of years ago, the bakery was located in a tiny space next to Street & Company and oftentimes would sell out of bread in the early afternoon. Now located below Fore Street in what used to be Nappi's Pizza and Pool, the new Standard is larger and supplies most of the city's best restaurants and stores with ample loaves while simultaneously fulfilling the public's retail bread needs.

Aurora Provisions, 64 Pine Street 871-9060

Located in a mostly residential neighborhood in the West End,

Aurora offers gourmet food prepared and ready for you to bring home. Or they'll heat it up in the microwave for your elaborate picnic. The wine, cheese, olives, pasta, oils are great here, too. Aurora also has a small café for lunch and desserts.

The Portland Public Market

When the Public Market opened in the fall of 1998, I had my doubts. Philanthropist Elizabeth Noyce's Libra Foundation spent $10 million to construct a massive 37,000-square-foot timber frame building with huge walls of glass on the corner of Cumberland Avenue and Elm Street behind the Portland Public Library. I thought it was too big and elaborate a scheme for a city with Portland's population. But Noyce believed the Public Market, filled with food and produce made and grown in Maine, would convince office workers, tourists and suburbanites to shop downtown. Unfortunately, Noyce died before the Market was completed.

Today, I'm a huge fan of the Market, stopping by a couple times a week for bread, vegetables, organic meats, free-range poultry and gourmet treats. Inside, it feels like a huge barn and smells like a chef's kitchen with chickens roasting and pies baking. The market is fun place for people-watching. Everyone is welcome, market managers say. Many of Portland's homeless hang here, surrounded by their plastic shopping bags filled with all their earthly belongings. Downtown yuppies grab quick snacks or a beer at the seafood café. Stylish suburban mothers sip coffee and nibble on baked goods while students from Portland High flirt and gossip with their friends working behind counters at Market stalls. And on cold winter days, the Market is warm and cozy, especially near the huge stone fireplace. Unfortunately the flames are gas-fed, not wood, but the effect is nice.

The Public Market has won several awards for design. I agree the building is interesting — especially for a new structure — but I can't get over the ugly 650-car parking garage on the other side of Cumberland Avenue connected to the market via Maine's first walk.

A.J. Kennedy's Fruit and Produce

For many years Kennedy's has supplied produce to Portland's finest restaurants. When the Market opened, they decided to get into the retail side of the business and they're doing a good job. The fruits and veggies are fresh at fair prices.

Horton's Smoked Seafood and Cheese Shop

Buy a quarter pound of the smoked mussels with garlic and wander the Market until the treats are gone. Then pick up a freshly baked baguette at Borealis Bread and return to Horton's. Buy a nice piece of triple crème (regular brie tastes like Velveeta in comparison) and scam a plastic knife from one of the vendors. Wander the market, spreading the superior cheese on the bread until both are gone. Repeat if you dare.

Stone Soup

Downtown soup devotees were elated when Stone Soup opened and the counter became instantly popular. The menu changes constantly, but the chowders, stews and consommés are always tasty. Stone Soup is a unique Market entity because it's nonprofit. The employees are chefs-in-training, working their way up from tough situations with help from the Preble Street Resource Center, Portland's best friend to the down and out.

Hanson Brothers Seafood and Café

Flounder piled high on ice next to weird-looking crabs. Oysters, steamers and littleneck clams just begging to be eaten. At Hanson Brothers, it's fun to look. Call me paranoid, but I'm not too excited about the bright sun shining through the glass window all day down on the seafood. In Maine, the rule is to buy the fish as close to the water as possible. I prefer Harbor Fish Market, down on Custom House Wharf, in the middle of the working waterfront. But I don't mind having a beer in the seafood café or enjoying the sometimes-complimentary mussels during happy hour.

Maine Beer and Beverage

Because of Maine's strict alcohol laws, drinking alcoholic beverages in the market is illegal (except in the café.) Too bad, because after checking out the selection at Maine Beer and Beverage, you can't help but get a little thirsty. Owned by a couple of lawyers, the store carries just about all the Maine beers sold in a bottle, plus some good microbrews from out-of-state. If you're more in the mood for vino, visit Miranda's Vineyard for a fine assortment of wine. Look in the cases on the floor for the best bargains.

Izzy's Cheesecake

My girlfriend and I once had an annoying hippie as an upstairs neighbor. One night he passed out with his stereo blasting the Grateful Dead. The CD must have been programmed to repeat, because we heard the same songs and extended jams over and over. Finally, we broke into his pad, which wasn't hard since he neglected to lock the door, and woke him up. I was very angry. He was apologetic, but I didn't care. The next day, he dropped off a large Izzy's cheesecake. Believe it or not, I forgave him. Izzy's is that good.

5

THE OLD PORT

I think there is a law requiring all tourists to visit the Old Port. The historic district is quaint, with plenty of cobble-stoned streets and 19th-century architecture. During the day, the brick sidewalks are busy with pedestrians browsing in the boutiques, antique, and book stores, galleries, and souvenir shops, occasionally stopping for lunch, ice cream, coffee, or an adult beverage while scouting possible locations for a fabulous dinner. And thankfully, except for a notorious Seattle coffee conglomerate, there is not a single franchise in sight. Bands perform free lunchtime concerts in Tommy's Park. Sidewalk fiddlers play for quarters and dollar bills. Waifish teenage girls try to bum money and smokes. And official "Downtown Guides" wearing safari-type hats give lost tourists directions to the public bathrooms in the ground level of the Fore Street parking garage.

The Old Port has a split personality. After sunset, the sidewalks fill with pub-crawlers and partyers looking for adventure. Fore, Dana, Moulton, and Wharf streets all have bars famous for rowdy good times. Yuppies and slackers check out pretty women in short skirts and halter tops. Hippies drink microbrews standing next to debutantes, fishermen, and off-duty bartenders. Frat boys and sorority sisters feel at home here. If a night of loud music, spilled beer, smoky bars, pool, darts, live bands, possible love connections, and an all-around drunken party sound like a good time, then head on down to the Old Port around 10 P.M. on any summer evening. In recent years, the police have beefed up their patrols, with beat-walking cops and mounted officers keeping the scene under control. But still the streets have a wild feel and the nightlife is unrivaled by any American city its size. (I know. I've been around.)

Shop till you drop

Until the early 1960's, only bums and winos partied in the Old Port. However, shrewd developers took notice of the desolate area and cheap property. They realized the 50 acres of run down and abandoned buildings between the downtown and the harbor could become a shopping destination. The first tenants were hippie artists, but over the years as rents went up, the artists were priced out of the business district. Today, dozens of independently owned boutiques selling knickknacks, toys, frippery and fine clothes for men and women are located throughout the Old Port. I'll highlight some of the groovy Old Port stores that Portlanders love.

Books Etc, 38 Exchange Street, 774-0626

Those behemoth book emporiums with coffee shops attached seem intent on forcing small independent bookstores to shutter their doors. That won't happen at Books Etc. Business is better than ever thanks to the personal service, the smart staff and the extremely cute dog named "Fly." Savvy Portlanders shop here because the clerks actually read the books they sell and can discuss them intelligently. The selection of children's books is second to none.

Northern Sky Toyz, 388 Fore Street, 828-0911

Kids and adults will have a fun time at this Fore Street toy store. In addition to a huge selection of kites ranging from the traditional to the most elaborate stunt kites, Northern Sky Toyz specializes in non-battery operated toys and games, plus yo-yos, wind socks and banners. Customers are encouraged to play with the toys and the staff is more than willing to show you the tricks. You might spot employees of the store flying spectacular kites at parks and beaches around Portland in order to drum up business. It works.

Amaryllis, 41 Exchange Street, 772-4439

Portland's most stylish women shop at Amaryllis for beautiful dresses, jewelry, shoes, and trinkets. The prices are moderate-to-expensive and everyone raves about the quality of the clothing.

Portmanteau, 191 Middle Street, 774-7276

If you're looking for a high-end, hand-sewn bag made from cotton, canvas, beautiful fabrics or leather, be sure to visit Portmanteau. The store also carries handmade accessories like check book covers, and jackets, coats and capes. All the merchandise is sewn on premises and is a good value.

Swiss Time Watches and Clocks, 86 Exchange Street, 773-0997

If your wristwatch battery dies or you inadvertently drop a chronometer in the ocean, head over to Swiss Time. The store offers minor adjustments on the spot and for major problems, full-service restoration is done on the premises. Swiss Time sells also trendy new and vintage watches, plus clocks of every type and size.

Condom Sense, 424 Fore Street, 871-0356

As you can probably guess, Condom Sense is well stocked with prophylactics, but that's not all this small, though not seedy, sex-related store sells. Many novelty gifts — including penis shaped pasta, inflatable dolls and other sex toys — are available here.

Amadeus Music, 332 Fore Street, 772-8416

Serious musicologists must visit this eclectic CD store located in the second-oldest building on the peninsula. Classical, blues, jazz, opera and world music are all available here. The staff is extremely knowledgeable.

Bull Moose Music, 151 Middle Street, 780-6424

Rock, rap, funk, metal, reggae, new stuff, old stuff, and country are all available at the Portland location of the small but growing chain of Maine-owned CD stores. Bull Moose supports the local music scene and stocks many recordings by local bands. The store also has a interesting selection of used CDs. A very fun place to buy music.

Videoport, 151 Middle Street, 773-1999

There is no better video store on the planet than Videoport. Over ten thousand films are available, including new releases, classics, indie productions, foreign flicks and the store's unique "Incredibly Strange Film" section.

What do teens do?

Despite the occasional harassment by their elders, Portland kids still have fun. Nightly during good weather, Post Office Park on the corner of Middle and Exchange streets becomes their chief hangout. Punks, hippies, jocks, slackers, the pierced and goths gather to flirt, gossip, and just be kids. The problem, however, is the cops usually close the park at 10 P.M. I don't know where they go next.

Lively libations

Our first settlers were rejected by Puritan Massachusetts because of excessive partying. Back in the early 1800s, most Portlanders were boozehounds. Parents drank with their kids. Ministers imbibed before preaching. Town officials required fortification prior to debate. Waterfront laborers took both morning and afternoon grog breaks daily. Liquor was in great supply and an economic force back then since Portland was home to a half-dozen distilleries that transformed West Indies molasses into rum. And tending bar was one of the few careers options for women.

A 19th-Century Scoundrel

Then along came Neal Dow, Portland's most temperate fool. In 1851, he persuaded the Maine Legislature to pass the first permanent law in the United States prohibiting the manufacture or sale of booze except for medical and mechanical purposes. Egad. Luckily, prohibition always fails thanks to human nature and the desire for mood alteration. Despite the ban, many Mainers still drank, brewing beer at home or buying firewater from bootleggers.

Despite his election as mayor of Portland, Dow wasn't popular with all the townspeople. Angry citizens tossed dead cats into his yard and splattered his house with nasty-smelling fluids. In 1855, the *Daily Argus* printed rumors that Dow had purchased a personal supply of liquor. Goaded on by the media, a mob descended upon City Hall. Actually, the city had bought $1,600 worth of medicinal booze, but the enraged horde didn't care. Dow further angered the crowd by brandishing a sword and ordering them to return to their homes. The angry throng stormed the building, intent on pouring the booze into the street. (Or taking it home for a nightcap.) Dow ordered the police to fire on the crowd. One man, a visiting sailor, was killed and five others wounded by bullets, bayonets, and bricks.

The *Daily Argus* wanted Dow to be put on trial, but instead a committee investigated and cleared Dow of any wrongdoing. In 1880, he ran for president as the Prohibition Party's candidate. Thankfully, he didn't have a chance.

Happy days are here again

Maine's anti-booze ordinances stayed on the books until 1934, one year after national prohibition ended. But this state just couldn't stop interfering with the sale of spirits. Today, under Maine law the government is the lone liquor wholesaler, setting prices statewide and levying a hefty tax, grossing $80 million annually from the sale of booze. While beer and wine are available at most corner markets, the hard stuff is only sold at about 200 "agency-stores" and the two-dozen state-owned outlets scattered across Maine. The Super Shop'n Save on the other side of Back Cove is an agency store and a 20-minute walk from downtown or jump on the #8 Metro Bus for a faster trip if you're desperately craving a bottle. Another agency store, RSVP at 887 Forest Ave., has the feel of a more traditional package store, but you need a car to get there. The local state store at 246 St. John Street is in the Union Station strip mall, across the street from the Greyhound station.

I've divided the bars into three categories: Pubs for tasting and talking; establishments; for rollicking good times and locations for anthropological studies of the mating rituals of the Old Port denizens.

Gay Bars

As far as I'm concerned, every bar on the peninsula is a gay bar because most Portlanders don't discriminate. That being said, the following four establishments are known as gay bars.

The Underground, 3 Spring Street, 773-3315

This is Portland's only gay nightclub. People come here to dance, especially on Saturday evenings when the floor is probably the most decadent in town. Buff guys often remove their shirts and everyone gets down and dirty. A very mixed crowd of gays and lesbians hang here and the Sunday night karaoke sing-fest has a strong following.

Sisters, 45 Danforth Street 774-1505

While everyone is welcome, this is a hot spot with the ladies. Many lesbians love to shake their booty here to Ani Difranco's sexy songs. On some nights it can really get rocking, other times you might be lonely. The outside patio is very comfortable place to hang out, especially for nonsmokers.

Somewhere, 117 Spring Street, 871-9169

This is a hole-in-the-wall neighborhood gay bar. It's not very fancy or classy, but the patrons have a blast. A piano player tickles the ivory and takes requests on Fridays and Saturdays. Somewhere is very popular with transgendered types. Tuesdays and Thursdays are hot nights for karaoke.

Blackstone's, 6 Pine Street, 775-2885

Another neighborhood pub, this a very comfortable and mellow bar where everyone seems to know everybody else's name. Shoot some pool or hang out with the loyal bunch of regulars who show up every night. While this is more popular with men, women are certainly welcome.

Cocktails with conversation

The following are my recommendations for a wide variety of local bars. Please note: These are merely in alphabetical order, not by preference.

Brian Boru, 57 Center Street, 780-1506

This Irish pub on the outskirts of the Old Port is also known as the Irish House of Pain. There's lots of blarney spoken here. Many of the regulars are charming folk and the happy hours are among the most popular on the peninsula.

Great Lost Bear, 540 Forest Avenue, 772-0300

The Bear is one of the best bars in Portland, but unfortunately it's off the peninsula. (About a $6 cab fare from downtown.) The Bear offers dozens of excellent microbrews on tap. The large horseshoe bar allows you to watch other patrons without them realizing you are spying on them. The menu is perhaps Portland's wittiest and the food is extremely tasty.

Gritty McDuff's, 396 Fore Street, 772-2739

Gritty's was Maine's first brewpub and remains a favorite with Portlanders of all types. The most loyal patrons own the mugs hanging above the bar. Most of the beer is brewed on the premises and I'm particularly partial to the brown ale. Bands perform a couple nights of the week and Gritty's is one of the few bars in town with a non-smoking section.

Mazza, 37 Market Street, 780-0800

Since Mazza opened in the summer of 1999, this Old Port lounge has been popular with 20- and 30-somethings pretending to act much older than their age. Mazza offers one of the best selections of single malt scotches and small-batch bourbons in the city (plus tasty small-plate appetizers including fabulous cheeses). A great place for intimate socializing.

Nappi's Pizza and Pool, 94 Commercial Street, 871-8030

This is the best place on the peninsula to shoot pool. Three coin-op tables are located on the first floor in the back. On the second floor, a half-dozen high end tables are for rent at six bucks an hour. With full bars on both levels, plus two different jukeboxes and good pizza (for a saloon), you'll always have a fun time at Nappi's.

Three-Dollar Dewey's, 241 Commercial Street, 772-3310

Dewey's feels like the bar in an airport hotel. But the beer selection is fabulous and there's lots of room to spread out. Be warned, the Friday happy hours are packed with yuppies.

Top of the East, 157 High Street, 775-5411

Located atop the Eastland Park Hotel, this lounge has the best view of any bar in Portland. Cozy in a 1970s sort of way, huge windows overlook the city and the bay and you expect a singer named Chicky to start crooning at any moment.

Una, 505 Fore Street, 828-0300

This is an extremely trendy hipster nonsmoking bar. The cocktails are super-expensive, especially the special martinis. The wine list is one of the best in the city, but don't even venture inside unless you're dressed to the nines.

Destinations for drinking draft

Amigos, 9 Dana Street, 772-0772

Many hip Portlanders have soft spots in their hearts for Amigos. They like to reminisce about all the crazy times they had there when they turned 21 or first moved to town. The place is often packed with sweaty and tattooed alternative types, especially on hot summer nights. Pool tables and dartboards are available.

Better End, 446 Fore Street, 874-1933

One of the best places on the Old Port to hear live music, the Better End's cover charge is usually quite reasonable. (Often just a dollar.) Sometimes the bar is packed with a dancing crowd. Other times, a lone weirdo will sway to the music of a band not ready to be playing in public.

Free Street Taverna, 128 Free Street, 774-1114

The Taverna is a favorite with a diverse mix of Portlanders. Gay, straight, greaser, slacker, artist, preppy, and redneck, everyone hangs here. Be sure to sample the Mighty Greek Ale, brewed by Bray's in Naples, Maine. There's live music seven nights a week at the Taverna and many of the top local bands play here often. Don't miss Bingo with Chicky Stoltz every other Sunday night.

Geno's, 13 Brown Street, 772-7891

Looking for a true rock'n roll experience? Visit Geno's, a Portland institution. Sure, it's dark, underground and a little bit dirty, but it's real, man. Famous musicians, including the Pixies, have played here and the bar is especially popular with eclectic punk-tinged bands. Geno the owner has been extremely supportive of local talent over the years and Portland musicians love him.

Stone Coast Brewing, 14 York Street, 773-2337

Upstairs at Stone Coast is probably the best place in town to see a live band. The beer prices are reasonable, the pool tables are playable and free on Sundays. Cigar smoking is encouraged here.

Zootz, 31 Forest Avenue, 773-8187

Those who fancy themselves "goth" or have a leather fetish should visit Zootz on Monday nights for the "Inquisition," an industrial dance party. Zootz is extremely popular with those who like to boogie to deejays spinning dance tunes from the 1970s, '80s and '90s. Live bands perform on Thursdays. Fridays and Saturdays, Zootz stays open until 3 A.M. for all-ages, after-hours dancing.

Hey Baby, What's Your Sign?

Fore Play, 436 Fore Street, 780-1111

Fore Play is supposed to be a sports bar, but except during football season, no one really pays attention to the 20 TVs on two floors. This is a perfect place to study the mating rituals of frat boys and sorority sisters. Plus you can usually find someone to challenge in darts, pool, foos ball, or air hockey.

Gilligan's, 42 Wharf Street, 773-9685

Apparently Wharf Street has become Portland's Tiki Bar District. Gilligan's is just like the Iguana (see below) without the dancing on the bar. Drunk people dance upstairs or outside on the cement patio.

The Iguana, 52 Wharf Street, 871-5886

Believe it or not, drunken women are encouraged to dance on the bar at the Iguana. And usually it's not a pretty sight. The bar's tropical theme might almost work in the summer when drinkers are wearing appropriate garb. But the rest of the year Mainers look ridiculous in trousers and heavy sweaters swilling pink intoxicants.

Dirty Bird and Shady Lady, 432 Fore Street, 780-0656

Two bars in one and the names don't lie. The popular Jello shots must give the patrons some sexual courage because the small dance floor is often busy with serious bumping and grinding.

The Pavilion, 188 Middle Street, 773-6422

If you're stuck in the 1980s, be sure to visit the Pavilion. Open on just Wednesdays and Saturdays, this dance club is Portland's version of Studio 54. Located in a former men's clothing store, the bar feels elegant and cheesy at the same time.

6

ON THE WATERFRONT

Portland harbor is beautiful and active, a mix of marine-related industry, bars, restaurants, and tourism and it's amazingly accessible to the public. On some bright summer days, the sky is extraordinarily large and blue and the bay is a calm mirror, reflecting the sun while seabirds squawk and brawl over the smallest scrap of food. Occasionally, you'll spot seals frolicking near wharves, diving deep for cover when boats approach. Trucks rumble along Commercial Street and park in the center lane to pick up and drop off packages to the dozens of shops and offices that line the street.

On foggy days, the harbor becomes a mystery, smelling of heavy salt air. Unseen vessels hidden by white vaporous shrouds blast foghorns, ominously announcing their positions while making their way up the shipping channel. Suddenly a ship appears like an eerie ghost, first with a mere silhouette, then unexpectedly illuminated by deck and running lights before vanishing, enveloped by fog. Wow. Wander the wharves, but stay out of the way of the hard-working laborers and sailors.

Portland's harbor prospers because it is a safe haven in rough weather. A trio of islands, Cushing, Peaks, and Great Diamond, act as a natural breakwater offering shelter from ocean surges and heavy northeasterly winds. During the winter, the waterway remains relatively ice-free, allowing vessels to cruise the shipping channel without worry. Year-round, boats of every color, shape, size, and rigging moor here and the port is popular with sailors from all over the world.

While the harbor has always been the heart of Portland, the ocean used to reach Fore Street, following the crooked shore. When the railroad boom began in the 1850s, the city fathers and the railroad barons decided to straighten out the waterfront by cre-ating Commercial Street, a mile long and 100-feet wide man-made thoroughfare. Train tracks ran down the center of the street con-necting the Grand Trunk and Boston and Maine Railroads. Portland became a transportation hub, linking Montreal to the sea via rail. The economy flourished and the trains covered the water-front with a thick layer of soot. But in the 1920s, Canada, intent on boosting its own ports, levied a hefty tax on goods shipped from America and Portland's bustling economy faltered. Over the years, the port slowly rebounded and now it is thriving once more, han-dling close to 17 million tons of cargo annually, almost a million tons more than the Port of Boston.

For your waterfront junket, start at the west end of Commercial Street and walk the length of the peninsula, ending up on the Eastern Promenade, rewarding yourself with sweeping views and treats.

The misnamed Casco Bay Bridge towers over the harbor from West Commercial Street. The drawbridge, which actually spans the Fore River to South Portland, not the bay, constantly reminds us of our dependence on the ocean by opening several times daily, most-ly during the morning and afternoon commutes. In the summer of

1997, the bridge replaced the so-called Million Dollar Bridge which was built for a million bucks back in 1916. Some locals miss the beautiful old bridge and its straight shot over the river and old style charm, but it was woefully outdated. Just months before the new bridge was finished, the oil tanker *Julie N* crashed into the Million Dollar Bridge, spilling over 100,000 gallons of petroleum products into the harbor. The old bridge simply wasn't wide enough to handle today's super-sized ships and had to go.

I love the new bridge, with a gentle curve halfway across the mile-long orange span, supported by imposing cement pillars. And at night when vessels need to pass, it's a spectacular sound and light show. Sirens blast, warning motorists of the impending opening, followed by clanging bells and dropping barricades adorned with flashing red lights to stop traffic. If you're lucky, an airplane preparing to land at the nearby Jetport will cruise by just above the massive draws reaching into the dark sky as a tanker, accompanied by a pair of tugboats ablaze with deck lights, passes underneath. And in the distance, the lights of South Portland shine brightly. In any weather, it's a wondrous sight, modern and ancient at the same time.

In the shadow of the bridge at the water's edge is the International Marine Terminal, owned by the City of Portland, and home to the M/V *Scotia Prince*. During the summer and early fall, this cruise ship makes daily trips to Yarmouth, Nova Scotia. There are just two reasons to go on the *Prince*: Either to save 858 miles of driving en route to a Nova Scotia vacation or to spend 24 hours gambling and drinking on the high seas.

Walking east on Commercial, you begin to get a feel for the city's grittiness and authenticity. Stop by Tiny's Bigman Seafood. Tiny the owner is proud of his girth and his fish are good and fresh. Another block east in the Industrial Welding Building you'll find Sub Sea Recovery. Greg Brooks is a former swimming pool installer and an adventurer who salvages shipwrecks. Someday he hopes to open a museum devoted to the sunken wrecks off Maine's coast.

At the head of Hobson's Wharf is Becky's, a great diner and a fun place to eat and eavesdrop. Head down to the Coast Guard Pier. A pair of 110-foot cutters are stationed here, though one is usually out to sea fighting the war on drugs and saving lives. Ask nicely and the Coasties are likely to give you a tour.

Do you like looking at fish? A group of Portland businesspeople want to build a $60 million aquarium on the waterfront that would focus on the aquatic life in the Gulf of Maine. We don't need it. Boston's aquarium, filled with exotic creatures, is a million times better than the proposed aquarium will ever be. Besides, we already have a place to view the region's fish. Visit the Fish Exchange at the

Portland Fish Pier. About 30 million pounds of fresh seafood is sold here annually to dealers who then ship the product all over the world. There's a daily auction Sunday through Thursday at noon. You're welcome to watch, but not to bid. After the auction, wander behind the Marine Trade Center to take a gander at huge fishing vessels refueling or undergoing dockside repairs.

By now you may be looking for a restroom. Across the street from the Fish Pier, at 305 Commercial, is the Visitor Information Center and public facilities. Walk on the north side of Commercial for a couple of blocks, then stop by Green Design Furniture to admire their high-end and handsome Maine-made tables and chairs. Many shops selling home furnishing, clothes and trinkets line the next couple of blocks. If you own a house, don't pass by Decorum, a store specializing in the stuff you'll never find at Home Depot.

Across the street you'll spot Union Wharf Market, a well-stocked mini-grocery with very tasty rotisserie chickens available for take-out. Walk behind the market, down to Union Wharf, past the gear shop and the lobster trap company. At any given time, you'll find fishing boats, harbor pilots, research vessels, and the *Maine Responder*, a ship whose sole purpose is to respond to oil spills. Turn around and get a clear view of the city. And in case you're wondering, the tall brick building with bricked over windows is an old cannery converted into self-storage units.

Heading back to Commercial Street, you'll find Sapporo, a Japanese restaurant with good sushi. Now it's time to check out a pier not included in any other Portland tour. Walk toward the water through the Fishermen's Wharf parking lot. You'll see some posh condos with balconies and sailboats in private slips. That's Chandler's Wharf and it's private. I want you to go next door to the right onto Widgery Wharf. Ramshackle and popular with the sea gulls, Widgery is bustling with fishermen unloading their catch or taking on bait. The wharf smells of work — rotten fish, seaweed and old rope. Mixed with the salt air, it's a sweet aroma to me, though not everyone agrees. The people living on Chandler's Wharf probably get used to the smell and to waking at five each morning to fishermen revving boat engines, warming up before heading out.

Walk back out to Commercial Street, grab a crab roll at the Bayview Restaurant and wander Long Wharf, a hot spot for water-bound sightseers. Here you catch a harbor cruise or water taxi; Long Wharf has a plethora of seagoing options. Whale watches, tours of the bay, sailing charters and private yachts-for-hire are all available here. Unless you're prone to seasickness, any trip is likely to be a good time.

Of all waterfront amusements, I highly recommend a trip aboard the *Lucky Catch*. Cruise with Captain Tom around Casco Bay in his real Maine lobster boat to haul ten real Maine lobster traps. Not only will you learn how our most famous crustaceans are captured in the wild for your dining pleasure, you'll actively participate in the hunt. As a former lobsterman, I wondered what kind of self-respecting fisherman would cater to a bunch of landlubber tourists, so I went for a voyage. Turns out Captain Tom is a genuinely nice guy and smart. In this era of trap limits and increased fishery regulations, he realized the need to diversify. Visitors fill bait bags with herring or measure and band lobsters while Captain Tom gives an informal history of the harbor and the fishing life.

Once you return to dry land, realize that only 35 years ago tourists and most Portlanders wouldn't have ventured to these parts of the waterfront. Back then, Commercial Street was a seedy, dangerous place overrun with rats and raw sewage floating in the harbor. But the late Tony Dimillo, a longtime Portland restaurateur, had vision and followed the lead of Old Port developers. In 1978, he purchased a dilapidated, burned-out coal pier and transformed it into Long Wharf and a full-service marina. Then he bought an old car ferry and renovated it into a 600-seat floating restaurant. Other developers became involved in the renovation fervor and the waterfront metamorphosed into visitor-friendly shops and eateries. Today Dimillo's is the state's busiest restaurant, serving hundreds of thousands of meals annually, though not many are sold to locals.

If you want to hang out with some locals, check out J's Oyster Bar on the Portland Pier. J's truly feels like Maine. Natives love this place because of the oysters, buckets of steamers, lobster, booze, and view from the parking lot patio. Plus, it's fun trying to figure out if the person drunkenly telling you stories is a millionaire lawyer or a panhandler.

Wander to the end of the Pier for more great views, but don't try following signs for the "Shore Way Trail." The trail never materialized. You could cross the street to have a drink at one of the watering holes affectionately named the Three Doors of Death. Years ago, the Commercial Street Pub, the Sail Loft, and Angie's were tough fishermen bars, but today they are mellow and fun in a gutsy sort of way.

Or if you're in a more historical mood, check out the Custom House. Leave it to the federal government to own one of the most ornate buildings in the city. Built in 1871 in the Italianate style, the upstairs has a 37-foot-high gold leaf ceiling. This is where sea captains used to pay their taxes with bags of gold coin. That's the reason for the balcony overlooking the room — armed men stood guard there. The building is still used by the Customs Service and the downstairs is occupied by the Coast Guard.

Directly across Commercial Street is Custom House Wharf, another pier worth checking out. Even if you don't need any seafood, visit Harbor Fish Market. You won't find better fishmongers in Portland. I buy lobster at Harbor Fish because the storage tanks are filled with flowing salt water from the ocean. I believe grocery store aquarium lobsters are sluggish and the meat is tougher.

Gilbert's on Commercial Street has creamy chowder and a nice deck out back. The seafood is good and greasy here and convenient for a quick meal before boarding a ferry. Or venture across the street to the Standard Baking Company.

Almost at the end of Commercial Street is the Maine State Pier and Casco Bay Lines. Almost a million passengers come through the terminal annually, headed to island homes or vacation. During the summer, the pier is often the site of special events and visits by tall-masted ships, cruise liners, and military vessels. Locals like to fish here for mackerel.

Please don't judge Portland's art scene by the 450-foot long whale mural airbrushed onto the wall of a building bordering the state pier. To me, it looks like a bad paint job on the back of custom van. But Wyland (he's such a big and famous painter, he has just one name) sold lots of souvenirs while painting the wall back in 1993. He has similar murals in other seaside cities across the country.

Next door is the Bath Iron Works shipyard and dry dock. Soon the facility will disappear because the company's lease is up. The most likely replacement will be a deep-water cruise ship terminal, big enough to handle the world's largest ocean liners. Currently, gigantic cruise ships like the *Queen Elizabeth II* have to anchor beyond Fort Gorges and ferry passengers ashore for port calls.

Now it's time for a little nature walk on the Eastern Promenade Trail. You can hike or bike along the shores of Casco Bay while taking in some of the most beautiful views in the world. The houses to your left are part of Portland's first neighborhood, the East End and Munjoy Hill. When using the trail during the summer or around the Christmas holidays, watch out for a little train occasionally belching black smoke. This is the Narrow Gauge Railroad with tracks just two feet wide running along the oceanside path. Ten or fifteen minutes of walking will bring you to the East End Beach, a great place to check out the sailboats riding the moorings or cruising the bay.

Climb the hill up from the water's edge to the Eastern Promenade for breathtaking views. On clear sunny days you'll have a sweeping panorama of Casco Bay, a dozen islands, an occasional lighthouse and the open ocean in the distance. On stormy days, the winds and tides turn the sea an angry gray. Then fog rolls in from the Atlantic, enshrouding the bay so quickly the islands vanish right before your eyes. But as long you're appropriately dressed, don't fear venturing out in a storm. There's an eerie, unforgettable beauty to the ocean during inclement and salty weather that makes the discomfort worthwhile.

PORTLAND DOWNTOWN

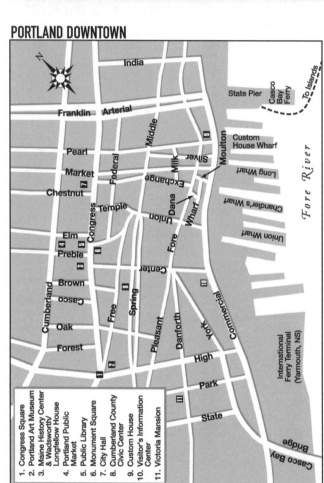

1. Congress Square
2. Portland Art Museum
3. Maine History Center & Wadsworth/ Longfellow House
4. Portland Public Market
5. Public Library
6. Monument Square
7. City Hall
8. Cumberland County Civic Center
9. Custom House
10. Visitor's Information Center
11. Victoria Mansion

7

GOING DOWNTOWN

Walking down Congress Street is the closest Maine has to a big city experience. Screaming sirens from police cruisers and fire engines echo loudly off the wind tunnel of brick buildings that line the street. Bike couriers dodge buses and delivery trucks. Panhandlers beg for spare change and bin tippers, the street name for those who collect cans for the nickel deposit, rummage through trash barrels. Maine College of Art students with multiple body piercings and hair of every color stand on the red brick sidewalks alongside downtown office workers taking smoke breaks. Bankers and businesspeople rush to important meetings past elderly Portlanders relaxing on park benches. Curious tourists point their cameras skyward photographing the distinctive 19th and early 20th century architecture.

Even at night Congress Street is busy. The location of several big city-type apartment buildings makes for steady foot traffic, by Maine standards, at all hours as people stroll the sidewalks. Some are drunk, stumbling home after an evening in the Old Port. Some work in the bars or other late-night gigs. And some are just lonely insomniacs out wandering.

Congress Street wasn't always bustling. Back in Portland's early days this area, a half-mile from the waterfront, was left undeveloped because it was too far from the harbor. After the British destroyed the city with a naval bombardment in 1775, the wealthier townspeople decided to build stately abodes on Congress Street, out of cannon range from future attacks from ocean-going armadas. Over the years, grand hotels and multi-story office buildings replaced some of those first homes and Congress became the city's focal point of commerce and government.

But disaster struck once Americans became addicted to their automobiles. Portland's population dropped as locals moved to the prospering suburbs. New retail centers sprung up outside the city limits. Urban blight hit the city hard. The once proud business center became an avenue of vacant storefronts. For almost 30 years, all the redevelopment schemes failed.

Then in the mid-'90s, the City Council renamed the area the "Arts District" and Betty Noyce purchased a chunk of downtown to revitalize it. Slowly, restaurants and shops filled the empty storefronts. In the office spaces above, high-tech companies, law firms, ad agencies and artist studios have great views of urban life. Several performance venues are located here and so are many of Portland's best galleries and museums.

The tour starts in front of City Hall across from the Congress and Exchange Street intersection. Designed by Carrere and Hastings, the same architects responsible for the New York Public Library, it's the third City Hall built on this location. The first was destroyed by the Great Fire of 1866 and its replacement burned in 1908. By 1912, the new, imposing City Hall opened with a 200-foot tall tower built with granite from North Jay, Maine. Take a walk inside to admire the elaborate staircase and details of the Second Renaissance Revival period. (There's a rest room on the second floor.) Check out the State of Maine room and the City Council chambers, dark and serious with polished wood and fancy lecterns. In addition to the standard governmental offices, City Hall is also home to the Merrill Auditorium, a recently renovated 1,900-seat performance hall. (More on the Merrill in Chapter 10.)

The city is run by a nine-member council led by a figurehead mayor. But the real power is wielded by the council's hired hand, the city manager. Taxpayers can thank the Ku Klux Klan for the city manager form of rule. Back in 1923, eager to eliminate the Irish Catholic and Jewish influence from Portland politics, the Klan heavily backed a referendum to abolish the board of aldermen and a mayor. In the days prior to the election, the Klan staged rallies, attended by thousands, claiming that cronyism would disappear under the new form of government. The measure passed. (That was the Klan's shining moment in Portland. It became inconsequential soon after.) Portlanders are satisfied with the arrangement. A recent effort to strengthen the mayor's job was rejected by voters.

Across the street from City Hall is the *Portland Press Herald*. You'd think the daily newspaper's proximity would mean extensive coverage of political goings-on. Alas, that's not the case. A block from the newspaper, on the same side of the street, you'll find Downtown Station, one of three Post Offices in the area. Cross Congress at the start of the commercial district to check out the architecture of the Masonic Temple at 415 Congress. Or take a gander at the back of Portland High School by walking down "Freshman Alley" around the corner.

At the Temple Street intersection is the beautiful First Parish Unitarian Universalist Church. Back in 1740, when Congress Street was still forest, Portlanders built a wooden meeting house on this site and Maine's constitution was drafted here in 1819. The current church was built in 1824 and is the city's oldest house of worship. First Parish is often open to the public, hosting "noon-day concerts," lectures and other events. Sneak a peak inside and don't miss the garden on the left-hand side of the church. It's a perfect picnic spot and quiet refuge from the downtown bustle.

Continuing down Congress you'll spot the Pierce Atwood Building, an 10-story monstrosity built in 1970 on the site of the old United States Hotel. At this spot in 1809, according to a plaque near this building, Portlanders were the first Americans to actually look at a caged leopard. The bank tower overlooks Monument Square, which is actually a triangle. "Lady Victory," Portland's bronze bombshell, a memorial to fallen Union Soldiers, stands watch over the brick plaza, providing pigeons a place to roost. During the summer, the square is abuzz with activity. It's a popular site for demonstrations and protests of all sorts. Evangelical preachers praise God here. Sidewalk musicians play for tips, sometime competing with lunchtime concerts regularly sponsored by the "Downtown District" or local radio stations.

Hungry? Monumental Pizza has good slices. Or enjoy a steamed hot dog from a sidewalk vendor, then people-watch. Check out David's for a slightly more formal, but hip, lunch, dinner, or drinks. Coffee By Design has strong coffee and other caffeinated beverages. And if you can't resist making photocopies while on vacation, Kinkos is always open in the storefront of the Lancaster Block, a six-story commercial building built in 1881.

Check your e-mail for free across the street at the top-notch Portland Public Library. Brown bag lunch lectures and author readings are often held here. History buffs should spend some time in the Portland Room on the second floor, learning more about the city's rich and sordid past.

Continue west on Congress, you'll come across the city's first skyscraper, now home to Maine Bank and Trust. Built for the Fidelity Trust Company back in 1910, it caused a stir with its revolutionary steel frame. No longer did the exterior walls have to support the building. Check out the gothic roofline and the smirking heads and intricate detail carved in the limestone. Cross Preble Street and the next skyscraper is the "Time and Temperature Building," so named for the trusty digital clock atop the roof. Portlanders love the Time and Temp, one of Maine's tallest buildings, because it is dependable, accurate, and visible from many points on the peninsula and the harbor. On snowy winter days the clock flashes *Park Ban* to warn residents to get their cars off the street or risk towing.

This section of Congress street is heavily populated with shops.

Both Material Objects and Encore sell excellent vintage and second-hand clothes for men and women. Levinsky's, a longtime Portland clothier, has good prices on casual clothes, sweaters, mittens, and hats in case you underpack. Fotoshops has film and camera supplies. If you ask nicely, the guys over at Second Option are sometimes willing to negotiate prices on their used appliances, furniture and miscellany.

History buffs must stop by the Center for Maine History and tour the Longfellow House. Built in 1785 by Peleg Wadsworth, Henry Longfellow's grandfather, it's the oldest residence on the peninsula. It's hard to imagine today, but when young Henry spent his childhood here in the early 1800s, he had a clear view of the tall-masted ships moored to harbor wharves. Now maintained by the Maine Historical Society, the brick house reminds you that even the wealthy had it rough back in the old days. Longfellow's mother often complained to her friends about the chilly rooms and drafty fireplaces. Be sure to check out the garden in back; free and open to the public, it's another urban hideaway perfect for a picnic.

The Maine History Gallery is also worth visiting. One recent exhibit provided a detailed look at the excessive boozing by Maine men, women and children back in the early 1800s. Another exhibit discussed and showed early Maine daguerreotypes and photographs, including death portraiture. (The technique of posing the recently deceased upright in a chair for one final picture.) Books about Maine, along with intelligent tourist trinkets, are for sale in the gift shop. Hard-core historians must check out the center's library where the smart staff of researchers are eager to help solve puzzling historic questions.

Continue west on Congress, if you stumble across a kid with green hair and piercings through every possible orifice, you're probably near the Maine College of Art. MECA (pronounced Mecca) put the art in the Arts District when the school took over the old Porteous Department store in 1995. A magnificent example of Beaux-Arts classicism built in 1904, look for the cute cherubic heads carved atop the limestone pilasters. On the ground floor you'll find the Institute of Contemporary Art and a gallery of student work available for purchase at reasonable prices.

Across the street, at the corner of Casco and Congress, the J.B. Brown Memorial Block begins. John Calvin Stevens designed the building in 1882 in memory of Portland's wealthiest capitalist of the nineteenth century. Delicate chimneys rise from the roof over asymmetrical windows. Many pedestrians completely miss the terra cotta details and fabulous brick works of this glorious structure. And none of them give a damn about the original Mr. Brown. What they really care about is one of the world's best shoe emporiums that occupies the corner storefront. Terra Firma has the hippest kicks in town for men and women.

For many people, a Maine vacation isn't complete without a visit to L.L.Bean. Luckily, Bean's opened a factory outlet on Congress in the old Five and Dime, so you won't have to battle the Freeport traffic. Right next door is Olympia Sports, which feels like it belongs in a mall.

Across the street is 547A Congress, another interesting Portland building, but not because of the architecture. The ground level is home to the Army recruiter, a hair stylist and a community policing station. The upper four floors are studios with high ceilings and great light where painters, photographers, sculptors, writers, and musicians ply their craft. Several other buildings similar to 547A line Congress Street.

Starving artists can't afford two rents so some give up their apartment because the studio is cheaper. (Some bypass the apartment route altogether.) They sleep on the floor or futon, sharing a bathroom down the hall and showering at the Y. (Some bypass the showering route altogether.) Unfortunately, it's illegal to live in these spaces zoned for work. Periodically, building managers make sweeps of the studios, evicting squatters. Then Portland's already tight, low-income housing market is flooded with a couple dozen poverty-stricken artists.

Continuing west on Congress for more shopping. Clay City is Portland's most eclectic store for funny little toys, pottery, ironic curios, and pornographic Mexican comics. The owner, Bruce, has a kiln out back. Don't bother him if he looks busy; otherwise, he's happy to chat. Amateur paleontologists should definitely stop by Stones' N Stuff, a store that sells rocks. For a beautiful and locally made bonnet or chapeau, check out the Queen of Hats.

From here you have a view of the offices of *Casco Bay Weekly*, the people who hired me to write this book. (Pick up a free copy and be sure to read Al Diamon, Liz Peavey, and Annie Sekonia's columns and all the latest info on the arts scene.) To the right is Aubergine, a fancy and pricey French bistro. To the left is the Clay

Oven, an inexpensive Indian restaurant. A couple storefronts down is Whit's End, a real neighborhood bar in a former bank. Be warned: Whit's End sometimes gets a bit rowdy, especially on karaoke night. But the patrons are very friendly and funny.

Now you're at the intersection of Congress and Forest Avenue at North Atlantic Leather, with coats, jackets, hats, bags, and anything you want in hides, run by an authentic longshoreman. A couple storefronts down is Paul's Food Center, the only real grocery store on the peninsula. Across Congress is A Maharani's Closet, a great second-hand store with a retro and exotic touch.

Congress Square, at the High Street intersection, is another example of Portland's thriving urban character. During the summer, downtown residents flock here. Tables and chairs are set up for dining and hanging out. A semi-translucent multi-colored awning stretches over most of the square. Kids run among the pigeons while office workers eat lunch. Occasionally, ne'er-do-wells sit on park benches to share a bottle in a brown bag and get a little rowdy.

On many summer nights, bands play on the Congress Square Stage. Sometimes it swings, sometimes it rocks, and there's always plenty of room to dance. WMPG (104.9 FM), Portland's community radio station, frequently broadcasts live talk shows here along with musical performances. One of the strangest Congress Square events I ever witnessed was the night *The Wizard of Oz* was shown on a large-screen TV in the square. I'm not sure who sponsored the screening, but the audience was hilarious. The film started late, so not a single kid was in the crowd. Anonymous in the darkened square, street people and hooligans, bar hoppers and slacker teens laughed, cried, and rejoiced together in Dorothy's madcap adventures.

Opposite from the square at the Congress and Free Street intersection is the almost triangular Hay Building, designed by self-taught Portland architect Charles Q. Clapp in 1826. The arched windows on the second floor are very Federal Period. John Calvin Stevens designed the third floor which was added in 1922. A Starbucks occupies the first floor tenant, the Hay Gallery and offices take up the second and third.

Across the Free Street intersection is the Portland Museum of Art and the Children's Museum of Maine, filled with interactive exhibits and a fun place to bring kids.

Opposite the square on the High Street side is the six-story-tall

State Theater building, home to a hundred offices and studios. Built in 1929, the interior has the feel of a noirish detective flick. Amazingly, not a single private investigator maintains an office here, but the tenants are a diverse group. An Eastern doctor is upstairs from a Jungian shrink. Mad painters and poets are neighbors to collection agencies. Jewelers and photographers share the elevator that occasionally smells like a home perm thanks to a hair salon catering to older woman addicted to long-lasting hair waves.

Need a haircut? The Columbia Barber Shop next to the entrance to the State Theater has been in business since 1929. The scene is very hip because the retro feel is completely authentic, down to the rotary telephone and ancient chairs. Next door is Drop Me a Line, specializing in gay and lesbian gifts and cards. And if you're addicted to vinyl, check out Enterprise Records with a huge selection of used albums.

Don't trust the clock tower atop the brick building on the other corner of High. It's beautiful, but the clock doesn't work. Notice the art studios above Tripp's Family Eyewear (a dependable place for minor repairs) with great big windows overlooking all the action. If you buy a piece of fine art while in the Portland, bring it to Artifacts next door, an excellent archival framer. If you're hungry for Vietnamese food, many locals enjoy Saigon Thinh Thanh.

The next several blocks on this side of Congress were mostly built in the early 20th century with storefronts on the ground level and apartments or offices above. Moose County is a skateboard and music shop always busy with alternative kids. Upstairs is Magpies, a reasonably priced antique store with occasional bargains and always good quality merchandise. Anna's has good deals on used furniture and second-hand oddities. Dance students learn new and old moves next door at Maine Ballroom Dance. The storefront window looks in on the dance floor. Need caffeine? I'd prefer you visit Coffee By Design's flagship store here rather than the trendy Seattle megachain down the block. Sun's Oriental Market is a clean and well stocked store with a selection of cookware in addition to all the fixings for sushi.

By now, you're probably wondering why all those crazy looking students are hanging out smoking and flirting in front of the red Romanesque church-like building across the street from Sun's market. It's the Baxter Building, the former Portland Public Library now used by MECA for a library, classrooms and home to the art school's photography department. James Phinney Baxter paid for the building, a gift to the city in 1888. Baxter was a five-term mayor and the visionary philanthropist responsible for Portland's extensive park system.

Continuing down Congress, we come to one of the most heavily populated blocks in the city. The old Lafayette Hotel on the left-hand side of the street was renovated into Lafayette Square several years back and now is a mix of subsidized and rental apartments. About 400 college students live across the street at Portland Hall, the downtown dorm for the University of Southern Maine. The collegians take a shuttle bus to the main campus a couple of miles away. Next door is the Trelawny building, another huge apartment complex, paid for by James Phinney Baxter. Across the street is Zinnia's, a very cool antique store in a very beautiful brick building, whose prices are sometimes negotiable. This whole neighborhood glows orange on clear days an hour before sunset.

In the shadow of the Trelawny Building is Joe's Smoke Shop, a Portland institution since 1945. Joe's is a peculiar place, the frequent site of a sidewalk comedy or tragedy. I shop here almost daily for newspapers, magazines, beverages, and an occasional visit to the largest walk-in, self-service humidor in Maine for a hand-rolled cigar. Employees make sandwiches in the back and sell plenty of porn, beer, wine, snacks, smokes, and lottery tickets. And now you've reached Longfellow Square, the west end of the Arts District, and home to the statue of the city's most famous poetic son.

This section of Congress has only recently become lively. Thanks to Local 188 and Café Uffa restaurants, the square has become a dining destination for local foodies and gourmand tourists. The Center for Cultural Exchange (see chapter 10) opened in 1999 in the site of a former dry cleaner and brings crowds of music fans. Cunningham Books has long been respected by bibliophiles. And if you're running out of cash during vacation, go try to sell a pint of plasma for 15 bucks at Portland Biologicals.

For the purposes of *Portland Undercover*, Longfellow Square is the west end of downtown. But make your own discoveries with further exploration. To your left are the Federal-style mansions of State Street with roads leading to the residential Victorian neighborhoods of the West End. And to the right is Parkside, a struggling neighborhood, battered by tough times and lousy housing, currently being renovated and revitalized.

Fans of beautiful old houses and architecture should definitely purchase Portland Landmarks' walking guide to Congress Street and the city and should also visit the Victoria Mansion (109 Danforth St., 772-4841). This Italian Villa was built in 1859 as a summer home for Ruggles S. Morse, a Mainer who made a fortune in the New Orleans hotel trade. If you think the outside is imposing — with its tower and stupendous ornamentation — you'll be blown away by the interior frescoes and elaborate woodwork.

8

THE GREAT OUTDOORS

Spend some time exploring our rocky shoreline or biking on island roads with amazing views. Play tennis, sunbathe at the beach, rent a kayak, or a paddleboat. Maine is filled with possibilities for outdoor adventure. In this chapter, I'll explain Portland's fabulous park system. I'll provide ideas for island getaways and day trips, plus hints for good times at fun local beaches. I'll furnish more options than you can handle. A tourist who can visit all the following attractions while on vacation should slow down and enjoy the view.

Picturesque parks

James Phinney Baxter was a smart and generous man. A pioneer in the business of food canning, Baxter made a large part of his fortune from selling canned corn and other vegetables to the Union Army during the Civil War. Wealthy beyond belief by his mid-30s, Baxter then turned his attentions to civic good and became active in charities. In 1893, Portlanders elected Baxter to the first of his five terms as mayor.

We should all be thankful Baxter went into politics; otherwise, we wouldn't have the many public parks and green spaces that dot the city. If it wasn't for Baxter's leadership and vision, the Eastern and Western promenades would not be the spectacular places they are today. Baxter stopped both proms from being taken over by private developers. He also spearheaded the expansion of Deering Oaks. And Baxter Boulevard running alongside and around Back Cove was his idea. Today, more than 900 acres of parks and playgrounds are green and fairly well kept.

Deering Oaks

Back in mid-1850s, the Deering family gave the city 54 acres (the site of a bloody Indian battle) in exchange for a tax break. By the turn of the century, Frederick Law Olmsted, the landscape architect responsible for New York's Central Park, designed the property into a pedestrian-friendly, multi-use park. In addition to the 200-year old oaks, which are perfect for napping under, the park is home to freshly renovated tennis courts and playing fields. Paddle boats are available for rental for a quick cruise around the duck pond.

Western Promenade

Back in the old days, the views from the Western Prom must have been pretty rustic, overlooking the Fore River, meadows, swamps, forests with mountain silhouettes. That's why the rich built their estates here in the late 19th century. They had no way of knowing the construction of the Portland International Jetport, tank farms, and the busy Interstate 295 would eventually spoil their view.

Despite the modern distractions, it's still a nice walk. On summer days, the prom is a popular luncheon spot. Workers from the nearby Maine Medical Center sit on the park benches in the shade. Mail carriers, many with their own lawn chairs, sun themselves, eat sandwiches and discuss postal politics. On some summer nights, sunset concerts are staged here.

Western Cemetery

Twelve acres of graves, crypts, grass and trees enclosed by a massive fence makes for a great place to walk a dog off the leash. Founded in 1829, this is Portland's second city boneyard. (Some of Henry Longfellow's family are buried here.) Today it's the only place in the city where dogs are allowed to run free. That bothers some people, offended by canines defecating near the row of Greek Revival Tombs. But most owners are responsible and clean up after their pooches.

Back Cove

Many years ago, this inlet was filthy with raw sewage and industrial waste. But thanks to environmental regulations, today the cove is clean and the three-and-a-half mile trail around the water is popular with joggers, walkers and bikers. And when the nearby spacious playing fields aren't being used by athletes, it's a fun place to fly a kite.

Mackworth Island

James Phinney Baxter instilled the spirit of philanthropy in his son, Percival Proctor Baxter. What the father did for the city, the son did for the state. A former governor, Percival gave Maine the 200,000 acres of wilderness that eventually became Baxter State Park. Percival also donated Mackworth Island, his family's Casco Bay summer estate, for the Baxter School for the Deaf. The school still calls the 15-acre island home, but you're welcome to visit and wander the shore and woods. The island is connected to the town of Falmouth by a long narrow bridge off Route One. Some locals like to fish here for mackerel, especially when the tide is coming in. And be sure to check out the pet cemetery, cared for in perpetuity, where Percival's beloved dogs are buried.

Interesting Islands

How many islands are there in Casco Bay?

Depends who is counting. In the old days, locals bragged about the 365 islands in the bay, but in reality the number is probably just over 750, counting all the ledges that are still visible at high tide. Those with a yearning for adventure should contact the Maine Island Trail Association (761-8225) for information on how to visit the small islands accessible only by kayak or small boat.

An Easy Excursion

Residents of the more populous Casco Bay islands count on the Casco Bay Lines ferries to deliver mail and supplies and to bring islanders to and from school and work on the mainland. But for you, the ferry is a cheap voyage around the bay. Bring lunch (and maybe six-pack or bottle of wine) and a book, then relax as the ferry embarks from the Maine State Pier and heads out past Fort Gorges, a pre-Civil War fort on a small island that was commissioned by Jefferson Davis before he became president of the Confederacy. Regular service is provided to Peaks, Long, Great Diamond, Great Chebeague, and Cliff island. Call 774-7871 for schedule and fares.

A Perfect Vacation

A couple of years ago, we rented a cabin on Cliff Island for a week for a mere 150 bucks. Granted, it didn't have running water and was dirty and decrepit with an electric toilet (don't ask), but we had a great time. To avoid the filth, we slept on the porch or under the stars. During the day we hiked island trails with astonishing ocean views and napped in hidden coves. At suppertime, we lit wood fires in the hibachi and grilled delectable meals, followed by games of cards while listening to music. Late at night, we took moonlit walks, occasionally startling a deer, then watched phosphorescent waves break on the shore. I'm not recommending you try to book this particular cabin (I wouldn't). But during our vacation we saw several fabulous cottages for rent. And most island homes have at least a couple of bedrooms. So if a place is going for $500 a week, it's a deal for a foursome or more.

Perfect Day Trip #1

For millenniums, natives have escaped to Peaks Island on hot summer days. They know the refreshing ocean breezes turn the beaches and green forests into a comfortable oasis. Luckily, these days Peaks is a mere 20-minute ferry ride away. Hundreds of summer cottages, often owned by the same families for generations, sit on the shores or nestled in the woods. About a thousand people live on the island year-round and many work in the city. After fifth grade, the kids attend city schools on the mainland.

The constant ferry service makes Peaks a convenient day trip. Pack your knapsack with a picnic and beverage and board the ferry at the Maine State Pier. After a 20-minute crossing, disembark and wander around Peaks' quaint little commercial district. Grab an ice cream cone the Peak's Island Café or check out the Mercantile, a gift store with a groovy thrift shop in the basement. Or visit the umbrella cover museum, the only museum in the world devoted to umbrella covers.

Rent some wheels from Brad's Bike Rental and Repair, then pedal off with the ocean to your right along the low, flat and appropriately named Seashore Avenue. Along the way, you'll spot some huge granite cliffs on another island about a half mile away. That's Whitehead on Cushing Island. Bike farther and Peaks' shore bends to the south, then east to the open ocean.

Ask a local for directions to Battery Steele, an old World War II bunker. Eat your picnic atop the Battery with tremendous ocean views then take a walk underground in the cavernous tunnels and hallways. If you're in town around the harvest moon in the fall, be sure to check out the Sacred and Profane. It's a one-day-only event (tickets are under $20) when a group of inspired artists take over the Battery with eerie visual installations, poetry rantings, "noise," and music performances. Later, partygoers feast on a sumptuous catered spread atop the Battery accompanied by a spell-binding moon rising out of the ocean and culminating with night of raucous contra dancing.

Or you can pedal back down to the ferry terminal in the late afternoon and return your bicycle then walk over to Jones Landing for cocktails on the spacious deck. This is one of the best places in the world to watch the sunset. Enjoy the view of a glowing Portland while drinking and dining.

Perfect Daytrip #2

Imagine yourself stretched out in a chaise lounge, growing tan on a sandy beach sipping a fruity tropical drink delivered chairside by a waiter or waitress. When you grow weary of relaxing, you shoot a game of pool on the outdoor table, play Ping-Pong or swap island stories with the mixologist behind the tiki bar. It's hard to believe you're in Maine. The cabana at Diamond Cove almost feels like a Caribbean resort. It's a resort and condominium community with a world-famous marina frequented by glamorous sailboats and yachts. Diamond Cove also has a fine restaurant with imaginative chefs known for creative cuisine and decadent desserts. This is one of the few Maine restaurants where people actually dress for dinner.

Back in World War II, Diamond Cove was known as Fort McKinley. Today many of the fine brick barracks and officers quarters have been renovated into high-end condos and single-family homes. Here's a nice weekend getaway: Three-bedroom townhouses with full-bath and Jacuzzi are available for two-day rentals at about $500. As part of the package, you get use of the swimming pool, tennis courts, and trails through the woods leading to private beaches.

Splendid seashores

Mainers don't really swim in the ocean. The water is just too damn cold. Lakes are better for swimming. Beaches are for the views and for walking, socializing, sunbathing, sleeping, reading, picnicking, people-watching, sandcastle building, Frisbee-throwing and just plain being lazy.

You can't go wrong in choosing a Maine beach. All have great views and are special in one way or another. The hours are generally sunrise to sunset.

A busperson's holiday

For those interested in remaining car-free and happy, take public transit to Willard Beach for views of ocean and island and take advantage of the great public access of the South Portland shoreline. Catch the bus, the older looking blue-and-white models on Congress Street head over the bridge and get off where Cottage Road turns toward Cape Elizabeth. Here you can grab a slice of pizza or sandwich at Dipietro's Market, which is also an agency liquor store. (I'm not suggesting bringing booze to the beach, which is illegal.) For a more refined breakfast or lunch, check out Barbara's

Kitchen. (Dinner is served Friday and Saturday nights.) And lovers
•
P
O
R
T
L
A
N
D

U
N
D
E
R
C
O
V
E
Rof fine art should definitely visit the Front Room Gallery and Zero
Station. The art openings and shows in the bright yellow storefront
are hip enough to make you forget that you're in suburbia. Owned
by Jon White, a talented ceramist and punk rock singer, the Front
Room shows a good mix of eclectic painters, woodworkers, photog-
raphers and sculptors.

Willard Beach is less than a 15-minute walk away. Follow the
street next to Barbara's Kitchen for a few blocks until you reach the
shores of Casco Bay. Here you will see islands and forts up close.
Cushing Island is to the right, House Island and Peaks are straight
ahead. The Diamond Islands, Little and Great, are more to the left.

Walking to the left toward Spring Point Light, you'll notice
something that looks like a university campus on the seashore. It is.
Students at Southern Maine Technical College are probably the
luckiest in the world when it comes to views. Feel free to wander
the campus or climb the rocky path out to Spring Point Light. Visit
the nearby Portland Harbor Museum and Gift Shop for information about lighthouse tours. Pay the two dollar admittance fee to
the museum (kids are free) and check out the small gallery devoted to the maritime history of Casco Bay.

This is also the site of Fort Preble which was completed just prior
to the War of 1812. Luckily, Portland didn't see any real action in
that war because the new fort's weaponry was hopelessly outdated
soon after installation. Today the fort is a fun place for a picnic
lunch and exploring.

Two wheels are sometimes better than four

If you're still not satisfied by the aforementioned destinations, I
recommend biking to the beaches. The ride is fairly flat and you'll
catch views that motorists generally miss because they speed by at
35 m.p.h.

Fort Williams and Portland Head Light Shore Road, Cape Elizabeth

While the actual beach is quite small and pebbly, Fort Williams
is a favorite with locals and visitors alike because of the wide-open
panoramas. The fort was an active military installation from 1899
until the late 1950s. Again, Portland was lucky not see any action,
especially considering the fort's original 1899 guns weren't replaced
until 1941. The town of Cape Elizabeth owns this awe-inspiring
oceanside park. Explore the paths leading to the ruins of old mili-

tary structures. Barbecue in the park-provided grills. Fort Williams is also quite popular with kite flyers, especially stunt-kite enthusiasts, because of the steady ocean breezes. And around the Fourth of July, the Portland Symphony Orchestra puts on a rousing patriotic outdoor concert complete with fireworks display.

Be sure take a picture or two of the Head Light, one of the most photographed lighthouses in the world. George Washington ordered the construction of the Head Light in 1787, one of the first commissioned by the new republic. Three years later when the lighthouse was finished, it was discovered that the tower wasn't high enough for the lamp to shine over nearby headlands. An act of Congress paid to make the lighthouse taller.

Over the centuries, the Head Light was rebuilt several times, updated and automated, all the while warning ships and sailors of the rocky coast and showing the way to Portland Harbor. Visit the museum in the former keeper's quarters for the complete history.

Two Lights State Park, Off Route 77 onto Two Lights Road, Cape Elizabeth

Two Lights is surrounded by craggy ledges, beautiful open ocean views, picnic areas, some fairly private behind shrubbery. Continue past the state park to the end of Two Lights Road to both lights and eat at the Lobster Shack. Open from April to mid-October, you would be hard pressed to find another restaurant with more sweeping views. Order a lobster or clams or chowder. Don't worry about looking like a tourist, you can't help it. The natives look like they're "from away" while dining here. That's because even the most stoic Mainer can't help gawking at the expansive view.

Kettle Cove, Route 77 S., past Two Lights Rd., left on Ocean House Rd, Cape Elizabeth

A favorite spot with locals. At high tide, follow the small wooden boardwalks through the marsh grass to a tiny inlet for warmed ocean swimming. Parking is free here and you're just a short walk from Crescent Beach.

Crescent Beach State Park, Route 77 South, Cape Elizabeth

A sandy stretch very popular with families, maybe because the bathrooms are better than at most Maine beaches. (Some beaches don't have any facilities.) Play on the swing set for some surreal ocean views. The little island off to the right is Richmond Island, home to the region's first European settler, the infamous scoundrel Great Walt Bagnall. At low tide, you can reach the island via a sandbar.

Higgins Beach, Route 77 South past Crescent Beach, Scarborough

A very popular beach with the inhabitants of the summer cottages and rentals that line the side streets leading to the shore. The waves can get quite big at Higgins, especially during storms, making the beach very popular with surfers year-round. Imagine that. Many people won't swim here even during the summer, but these diehard surf nuts love the winter waves. (Of course they wear wet and dry suits.)

Scarborough Beach, Route 77 South to Route 207, Scarborough

I don't know anyone who doesn't love Scarborough Beach. It's huge. It's sandy. The open ocean seems so vast and immense here. Makes you feel almost insignificant. This might cheer you up. Parking is just three bucks and yet the beach is surrounded by some of the most expensive real estate in Maine. What a bargain!

Ferry Beach, right off Route 207 onto Ferry Road, Scarborough

Take a look at a tide chart before heading out to Ferry Beach. At high tide, there is very little sand, but when the tide goes out, you can walk forever. Ferry Beach is preferred by same-sex couples because of the very relaxed and accepting atmosphere. And some locals highly recommend the beach for late-night skinny-dipping. Parking is five bucks.

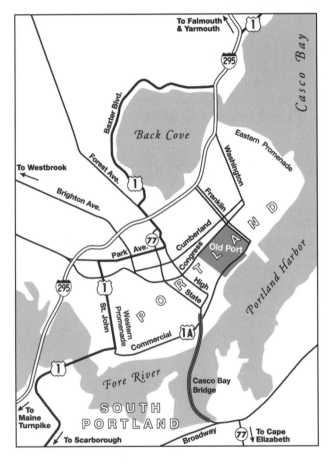

HOW TO GET LUCKY IN PORTLAND

Why does a guidebook about Portland have a chapter on sex? In New England we generally don't like to talk about such private deeds. But this Yankee city has always been a town for swingers. Perhaps the salt air has aphrodisiac powers. Looking back at the almost 400 years since the white settlers arrived here, a pattern develops. Some locals pursue erotic endeavors while others scold them for immoral behavior. It was true in 1650 and it's true today.

The old-time Portland histories only hint at the lascivious actions of the early residents. But considering most of the European colonists living in Maine fled the uptight Puritan communities of Massachusetts, this was undoubtedly a passionate place. Historian William Willis refers to hundreds of court cases in which defendants were charged with fornication.

There's no record of when the world's oldest profession got its start in Portland. The first harlots and jezebels probably showed up soon after the wretched white men. And as the harbor grew into an important shipping port, drunken sailors arrived after long months alone at sea, hungry for companionship. Carnal desires were satisfied in easy-to-find brothels and alleys. These lusty street crimes were infrequently prosecuted until the first police force was organized by the mid-1700s.

But in the 1820s, life for the working women became tougher. A new red light district had sprung up on Munjoy Hill, also known as Mount Joy Hill by some because of all the brothels on Larch and North streets. The cops cracked down, arresting streetwalkers for a variety of offenses, although not prostitution. (This was New England. Such charges would have been indecent.) Some of the more righteous citizenry were angered by the decadence and began publicly insulting and attacking the prostitutes. The women suffered at the hands of their clientele as well. Violence-prone sailors were quick to resolve conflict via a vicious beating.

In the following decades, self-righteous prudes began their ascent to power. But even while Neal Dow and his prohibitionist posse were preaching the evils of drink, the peddling of flesh and firewater still thrived. The upper floors of several Old Port buildings were the locations of popular brothels. But the real boom times didn't hit until World War II.

War is always good for business. The battles in the European theater helped Maine escape the poverty of the Depression. The Atlantic Fleet, and thousands of sailors and merchant seamen, were stationed here since Portland Harbor is the closest major port to Europe. And the Allies, desperate for cargo vessels, pressed two Casco Bay shipyards into around the clock service. At the height of production, some 30,000 workers (including 3,300 female "Rosie the Riveters") were busy building 13 Liberty Ships at any given time.

But the waterfront and Old Port were still seedy and dangerous and popular with disreputable and nefarious types. Hundreds of young female runaways came to Portland looking for love, or at least money. Some became prostitutes in brothels, others sold themselves in alleys. Many were merely amateurs. Of course such swinging doesn't go unpunished. Health officials reported a huge outbreak of gonorrhea cases. Believe it or not, the military exonerated the professionals as the cause of the epidemic. The working women knew how to protect themselves. Sadly, the inexperienced young girls were the primary carriers of the sickness.

Today, professional call girls carry pagers and cell phones and freelance for escort services. Now only the most desperate hookers work the streets, mostly on a depressing block in the Parkside neighborhood. And their johns are sleazy types, looking for cheap, quick thrills. The cops routinely run sting operations. (The better-looking streetwalkers are usually undercover cops.)

Although modern Portland is relatively safe and pure compared to the old days, our police department still acts like the streets are busy with vice and corruption. In recent years the chief has cracked down on graffiti, youth gangs, newly released ex-cons, and panhandlers. If you ask most Portlanders, none of those issues would qualify as pressing.

The chief's only victory, a minor one at that, was eliminating a Congress Street porn theater. About five years ago, officers raided porn shops, corner markets and legitimate video stores, confiscating magazines and movies. A big press conference was held at the police station where reporters were shown clips from S&M videos and allowed to peruse porn the chief thought to be unfit for public consumption. Summons were handed out and the merchants paid fines.

Then *Casco Bay Weekly* ran a news story about public orgies and unsafe sex taking place at the Fine Arts Cinema. Officers investigated and started arresting theater customers engaging in lewd conduct. Theater management was ordered to install a surveillance camera and monitor the activities or shut down for good. Quickly the frisky patrons found other locations to pursue their horny hobbies. Eventually the Fine Arts closed.

The chief's other pet peeve is people cruising for anonymous sex on the Western and Eastern promenades by sex addicts looking for an anonymous erotic encounters. So the city passed a no-cruising ordinance. Signs were posted warning of arrest for those spotted repeatedly making rounds in their sexual search. (I still wonder about the constitutionality of the law.) But cruising, I hear from those in the know, is still quite popular.

Two sex shops in Longfellow Square — no puns please — survived the war on porn and are as busy and profitable as ever. Both establishments have video-viewing booths in the back. Rumor has it that sometimes more than one person occupies a booth, but there are signs warning against such practices.

Video Expo, 666 Congress Street, 774-1377

It's easy to identify the pedestrians headed into the Video Expo. They're the ones looking furtively before approaching the porn store. Inside, behind the blacked-out door and windows, it feels like a regular video store, until you take a look at the movies. This is serious hardcore porn. The store also sells artificial penises and vibrating love toys of every shape, color and size.

Treasure Chest, 2A Pine Street, 772-2225

Located on the other side of Longfellow Square, this porn shop is sleazier then Video Expo, but it's more popular with women. Don't ask me why. The Treasure Chest stocks similar sex toys, but management need to work on the displays. Everything just seems so disorganized.

Mark's Showplace, 200 Riverside Street, 772-8033)

Portland's lone strip club isn't even on the peninsula. Mark's is clean, upscale, expensive and home to America's only topless donut shop. I'm not joking.

10

CULTURAL ENDEAVORS

This may sound like sacrilege to some Portlanders, but I don't believe Henry Wadsworth Longfellow was a great artist. In fact, I find his poetry trite and almost childlike. I'm not the only one that thinks so, either. At the time of Longfellow's death, Walt Whitman wrote, "He is not revolutionary, brings nothing offensive or new, does not deal hard blows." In other words, he's a poetic lightweight.

But he was famous in his time. And for Portland, that's good enough. Besides his statue in his square, you can take an interesting tour of his childhood home. Or visit the geniuses behind Longfellow Ale. A city elementary school, an arboretum and a laundromat all bear his name. But Portland Undercover, unlike every other book and brochure about this city, will not include a single line of his poesy.

My favorite Portland poet is a madman named Russ Sargent. His magnum opus, called *Clarion Vice*, consists of dozens of vivid cantos committed to memory. Someone should give this man a gig on TV or Broadway. (In real life, he's a funny, friendly genius.) Catch his act at local poetry readings, occasional island events and sometimes beneath the Casco Bay Bridge, where he rehearses among cement pillars and steel girders.

Hundreds of gifted people live in this city. Photographers, painters, printmakers, metal-smiths, jewelers, poets, novelists, and musicians call Portland home. They toil away, usually in anonymity, in studios along Congress Street or in attic garrets.

Depositories of viewable representations

The Portland Museum of Art, 7 Congress Square, 775–ARTS
The PMA is amazingly well stocked with masterpieces by Renoir, Rodin, Degas, Cassatt, Monet and Picasso. The museum, designed by I.M. Pei and Partners, also houses a fine collection of the famous artists that lived and painted in Maine. Admission is six bucks, but savvy art lovers visit the PMA for free on Fridays between 5 P.M. and 9 P.M.

The Institute of Contemporary Art, 522 Congress Street, 879-5742
Located in the street level of the Maine College of Art, this is a gallery devoted to living artists. The ICA often shows cutting edge work in visual, conceptual and performance art. Free and open to the public.

Gratifying galleries
Looking at brochures for Portland, I find a couple dozen art galleries listed. Alas, some of these establishments are merely frame shops but discerning connoisseurs of cutting edge work at very reasonable prices will be happy with the following galleries.

Local 188, 188 State Street, 761-1961
Local is the best gallery in the state for astonishing paintings, photography and sculpture. Run by a trio of artists, the shows are sometimes funny, sometimes sexy, and always provocative.

June Fitzpatrick Galleries, 112 High Street, 772-1961
June Fitzpatrick is a heroine to many local artists. Not only does she show interesting art, but her connections with collectors translate into sales. Her original space on High Street shows more established painters and sometimes sculpture and other media and her newer Alternative Gallery on Congress Street is devoted to emerging artists.

Delilah Pottery, 134 Spring Street, 871-1594
Run by one of the nicest and zaniest people in Portland, this West End storefront is chock-full of beautiful objects that used to be lumps of clay. The gallery, though small, frequently shows vivid paintings by local artists.

Hinge, 576 Congress Street, 761-9552
This storefront gallery primarily focuses on work from talented artists of color and women. This is also one of the few establishments in Portland that carries local 'zines and handmade books. Poetry readings and puppet shows are occasionally held here.

The Hay Gallery, 594 Congress Street, 773-2513
Many of the area's most gifted artists are shown here. The problem, however, is that the space is so jam-packed with pieces that you don't have enough room to get a decent perspective of the more interesting work.

Danforth Gallery, 34 Danforth Street, 775-6245
Staffed by volunteers, this nonprofit space is devoted to Maine artists and run on a shoestring. Lectures and discussions about local history and art, are often held here.

Greenhut Galleries, 146 Middle Street, 772-2693
This is the probably best place to see art in the Old Port. While not known for being hip, Greenhut has a talented roster of painters and sculptors. Plus they do high-quality archival framing.

Salt Gallery, 110 Exchange Street, 761-0660
The gallery is on the ground floor of the Salt Institute for Documentary Studies, a college-accredited program where writers and photographers work together on documentary projects linked to Maine.

Dazzling dance

Ram Island Dance and the New Dance Studio, the two leading modern troupes, regularly present new work and interesting world premieres. Ram Island is unique because the principal trio of dancers hold salaried positions and all three had professional careers in New York City. The two local ballet companies, Portland Ballet and Maine State Ballet, present several performances annually. The city is also home to a talented group of Scottish dancers and to Baraka, a belly-dancing troupe.

Tantalizing Theater

The most exciting stage performances in Portland won't be found in the professional theaters. Out of Cake and the Bastard Sons of the Infocaplyse are two of my favorites companies that irregularly offer theatrical entertainment. The Children's Theater of Maine, located off the peninsula at 716 Stevens Ave, is also known for staging compelling work starring talented kids.

To Catch a Flick

The Movies, 10 Exchange Street, 772-9600

The owners have an eclectic and intellectual taste, frequently showcasing work that otherwise might not make it to a Maine screen. The Movies also supports local filmmakers.

Nickelodeon, 1 Temple Street, 772-9751

Very popular with teenagers, the Nick, an Old Port multiplex, is a 21st century anomaly: Tickets are amazingly priced at just $1.50.

Keystone, 504 Congress Street, 871-5500

Have dinner and a movie at the same time. The comfortable seats make three-hour movies almost bearable. The popcorn is free and beer and wine are available. The Keystone frequently screens independent films and is also supportive of local moviemakers.

Harmonies and melody

From smoky bars to an elegant concert hall to active houses of worship, Portland has an remarkable number of venues for a city of this size.

Merrill Auditorium, 20 Myrtle Street, 842-0800

Located within Portland City Hall, this 1,900-seat auditorium is a fantastic place for concerts and most patrons like to dress up for a night of culture. In addition to regular performances by the Portland Symphony Orchestra, organ concerts, and local ballet companies, the Merrill also hosts big-name jazz, blues, opera, and touring Broadway shows.

State Theater, 609 Congress Street, 775-3331

If the Merrill is for music lovers who wear fine clothes, then the State is for those who prefer torn jeans. Built in 1929, this grand old movie house is now geared towards massive throngs of 1,500 sweaty concertgoers. Dylan played here a couple of times. Meatloaf, George Clinton, and Soul Coughing have also put on roaring shows here.

Center for Cultural Exchange, One Longfellow Square, 761-1545

With help from the city, corporate donations, and grants, the nonprofit Center for Cultural Exchange opened in 1999. As the name implies, this venue brings musicians and dance troupes from all over the world to Portland for performances, workshops, and educational programming.

Bands and bars

The following saloons are possible locations for hearing good local bands: Free Street Taverna, Better End, Geno's, Bramhall Pub, Asylum, The Skinny and Stone Coast for rock and eclectic music. Check out the Big Easy and the Breakaway for blues.

The Munjoy Hill Society is my favorite Portland band. Its talented and original hipsters have a blast playing and it shows. Everyone loves to dance to its tunes, ranging from mambo to lounge to rock to salsa.

Anti-Friend Hut is Portland's only Dadaist performance group. These jokers dress up in cardboard robot costumes and play "noise" with a variety of instruments, including drums, fiddles, snow shovels, random pieces of steel and a microphoned tricycle. Rarely do they play indoors because their antics are far too wild. These fellows can often be found performing near Longfellow Square prior to art openings at Local 188.

Cerebus Shoal plays long and bizarre rock songs, some lasting more than a half hour. The group's infrequent local performances are very surreal and experimental.

Here are some quick descriptions of other talented locals bands: The Coming Grass plays modern, thinking person's country-rock with melodious singing, guitars, and drumming. The Jerks of Grass are a great bunch of ragamuffin musicians with fiddles, mandolins, other string-instruments, and a love for bluegrass. For stupid punk pop with heart, check out Peep Show. Surf-a-billy specialists Shutdown 66 always put on good — but infrequent — shows. Fans of modern-disco-pop-should not miss Tin-Tin's Rocket. For straight-up indie guitar rock, be sure to catch Lincolnville. Another great band in the alternative vein is Spouse. Twitchboy is bound to please those who enjoy a mix of rock, rap, and metal. And you can't talk about Portland's music scene without mentioning the Rustic Overtones. The major label debut of Maine's most famous musical sons — with special guest David Bowie singing backup on a couple of tunes — was expected to be released by Arista in the spring of 2000. (Bowie said he loved the horn section.) When these boys play Portland, it's a pandemonium-filled party and standing room only.

11

WHERE TO NEXT?

I rarely stray from Portland's three-and-half-mile peninsula. But since you're on vacation, you may want to check out the rest of our beautiful state with its countless amazing views and natural phenomena.

Yarmouth, Nova Scotia
12 hours by sea

Under the Casco Bay Bridge on Commercial Street is the berth for the M/V *Scotia Prince*. (1-800-341-7540) During the summer and early fall, the cruise ship/car ferry makes daily trips to Yarmouth, Nova Scotia. People take the *Prince* either to save three days driving to Halifax or to drink and gamble in the 3,600-square-foot casino. You can't bring your own booze, but duty free liquor is available for purchase at a decent price for consumption onboard.

Boothbay Harbor
60 miles northeast of Portland

Anytime you drive on Route 1 after Memorial Day expect some serious traffic. But once you get into Boothbay Harbor you can relax. The hiking trails through the nearby pine and cedar forests are great fun to explore, especially when you stumble upon fabulous views of rocky shoreline and the mouth of the Damariscotta or Sheepscot Rivers that flow into the Atlantic Ocean.

Midcoast Maine
80 miles northeast of Portland

Rockland is my second favorite Maine city. It's a smaller version of Portland, with an active seaport and fisheries, without as much culture, and fewer rich people. Vinalhaven, a fairly large island with an interesting fishing village, is a short ferry ride away from Rockland. Penobscot Bay is popular with sea kayakers who are warned to avoid the busy shipping channel. A little further north are the towns of Rockport and Camden which are jam-packed with tourists all summer long.

Bar Harbor, Acadia National Park and Mount Desert Island
161 miles northeast of Portland

For stunning ocean views from mountaintops be sure to visit Acadia National Park. Pemetic Mountain is just a mile walk to the ridged summit from a parking lot. The more famous Cadillac Mountain is busier since the summit unfortunately can be reached by automobile. The better Acadia vacation is spent biking on the 50 miles of well-maintained carriage roads overlooking cliffs. Hikers will enjoy the many trails. Be sure to visit the fishing communities of Northeast Harbor and Southwest Harbor.

Baxter State Park and Katahdin
222 miles north of Portland

The 200,000 acres of wilderness donated to the state by former Governor Percival Baxter makes up the largest tract of land east of the Mississippi forever protected from development. Katahdin, at 5,267 feet, is Maine's tallest mountain and towers over the park's southeast corner. Rare floral and fauna for the region are found throughout the park and the mountain. The park has 10 campgrounds, including two accessible only by foot, but be sure to make reservations.

Skiing

Each year, more than a million skiers make their way down Maine's mountains. For downhill skiing, you have many options, but be sure to stop in Portland on your way to or from the high country.

Sugarloaf/USA in Carrabassett Valley, about two-and-a-quarter hours from Portland, boasts over 100 kilometers of groomed trails. The beer is good, skaters can use the Olympic-size rink and full rentals are available.

Sunday River is about a 90-minute drive from Portland, making it very popular for day skiing trips. With 126 trails on eight inter-connected mountain peaks (and one of the largest snow-making operations in the East), there's skiing available for every skill level.

For a smaller mountain but incredible panoramas of Penobscot Bay, try the Camden Snowbowl about an hour and half drive up the coast. Camden has several great inns and good restaurants that remain open during the winter months. The 1,300-foot Ragged Mountain has 11 trails, many with great views of offshore islands.

Maine is also home to several other smaller ski areas including Mount Abram in Locke Mills which has very reasonable lift ticket prices. Shawnee Peak in Bridgton is about a 45-minute drive from Portland. And though it's a small mountain experience, Lost Valley in Auburn is just 35 miles inland.

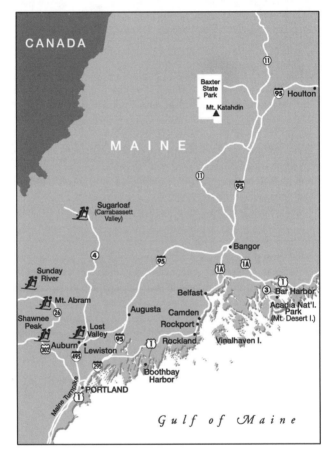

CANADA

Baxter
State
Park

Mt. Katahdin ▲

(11)

(95) Houlton

M A I N E

(11)   (95)

Sugarloaf
(Carrabassett
Valley)

(4)

Sunday
River

Mt. Abram
(26)

Shawnee
Peak

(302)   Auburn
(495)   Lewiston

Lost
Valley

(95)

Augusta

● Bangor

(1A)   (1A)

Belfast ●

Camden
Rockport ●

(1) Rockland

(1)

(295)

(1)

Boothbay
Harbor

Maine Turnpike

PORTLAND

Vinalhaven I.

(1) Bar Harbor
(3)
Acadia Nat'l.
Park
(Mt. Desert I.)

Gulf   of   Maine

In Conclusion

By now, you've probably guessed that I love this city. While providing countless tips on how to have a great time in Portland, I didn't share everything. We didn't discuss the Feast of Saint Rocco or the fascinating political debates at Vespucci's or the craziness of Bubba's Sulky Lounge. And I didn't have enough room for the legends of Len's Market or other great peninsula sagas. I barely mentioned the Southside, the world's best neighborhood, where we smell the salty ocean and listen to the long song of ships' whistles on foggy nights. And I didn't try to explain the sunrises and sunsets with violent pinks and purples that reach across textured open heavens, inspiring artists with ethereal light. Visit with your eyes open and you'll discover these wonders and many more.

Our cityscape is in a constant state of flux. Businesses open and close. Buildings get sold and renovated. Occasionally fire strikes. Don't blame me if something I discussed no longer exists by the time you get here. But the tides will always rise and fall and you can always have fried clams for dinner. This is a place where if your dog disappears, everyone is out looking. A city of warm summer days with gentles breezes and winters of snowbanks, icy sidewalks and bitter winds.

In some ways, the peninsula is a microcosm of America in these boom times, without the chain stores and strip malls. But I like to think that Portlanders are different than the norm. We're cantankerous and self-righteous and often times contradictory. We can't figure out if we're a small city or a big town. While we embrace the modern, it's still bothersome to see someone talking in public on a cell phone. We don't hail cabs here. If you need a taxi, check the yellow pages or head on down to the front of Paul's Foods. This isn't New York or Boston. In Portland you can smile and say hello to passersby without feeling as though you broke the law. Have a great time.

• • • • • • • • • • • • • • • • •